*Where Trout Sing*

# Where Trout Sing

### And Other San Francisco Stories

## Art Dollosso

*Foreword by Russell Chatham*

San Francisco 2012

Library of Congress Control Number: 2012902469
Dollosso, Art.
Where Trout Sing and Other San Francisco Stories / Art Dolloso – 1st ed.
p.    cm.

ISBN: 978-0-578-10237-5
I. Fishing.    I. Title.

Sonoma Small Press
Printed in the United States of America

First Edition

These sketches are dedicated to my father
Alfredo Dall'Ozzo and his two brothers,
my uncles Guido and Giovanni, who gave
me guidance and an unquenchable
thirst for all things outdoors.

Memory is the diary we carry with us.

—Oscar Wilde

# Contents

# Contents

# *Foreword*

If the right coast of America is Mars, then the left coast is Venus.
People who think only on Mars has anything happened which
matters, may wish to review some evidence to the contrary in Art
Dollosso's book which broadly swings historically from real laughs to
real tears. Those of us who grew up on Venus will be quick to
recognize the authenticity of its ironies as well as its tropic of
heartbreak, a narrative ride worth ten times the price of admission.

Russell Chatham
Marshall, CA

# *Preface*

When I was a very small boy I received a fishing rod that had a former life. It had been a Christmas tree, a Douglas fir that had graced our living room that past winter. The tree had been stripped, sanded, shellacked and reconfigured as an angling instrument by my struggling father, who, as near as I could tell, was brought up on bad news. It was a fishing rod that any leg breaking racketeer would have been proud to use on a business trip.

The rod followed me around, about and all over San Francisco Bay, just like Lassie. Piers, promontories and points were my specialty. When I was a little older I'd go out to Ocean Beach and fish for striped bass from dusk till dawn. I'd watch the surf casters throw lures up towards the moon and out over the breakers by firelight. Fires were everywhere we fished at night—bonfires, big ones. Although those times are fifty years astern, I still find myself by campfire light, sometimes on the Sacramento River watching First Nation Wintuns slip dip nets into the dark waters. All anglers exchange stories around a fire, and the stories they told, and that I heard, were more illuminating to me than any fable about an enchantress living in a forest filled with gnomes ever could be.

I suppose you could say that those fireside stories sparked a small flame inside me that was fanned by the remarkable coastal breeze that continues to carry folks here from all over earth. It's a wind, unlike any other, that permits us all to settle down, take root, and feel at home.

A life, or a book on the sporting life, should certainly orbit around the accompaniment of *la famiglia*, acquaintances, and friends.

I give the most affectionate of nods to my wife Trudy, for her deep devotion and her affectionate companionship that allows the two of us to live a life like the best romantic comedy movie you've ever seen.

I want to thank Danny, my son, for giving me that most precious gift of all. Time together. To my son Vic and my daughter Julie, many thanks for our treasure trunk full of "remember whens."

These days, Michael "Mac" MacWilliams and his family grace note my sporting life like the finest *Field & Stream* story ever told. Mac is an ace in all he attempts. Without his encouraging advice and *au point* editing these stories may as well have been written on the wind.

Most of these remembrances are from memory, others have an outside assist from imagination. I sure hope that readers somewhere, everywhere, can sense the tang of salt sea air permeating through these pages, and smile.

Art Dollosso
Sonoma, CA

*Where Trout Sing*

# That First Fish

Lets begin at the beginning: San Francisco, circa the late '40s to early '50s. The young future fishermen of the city begin their angling odysseys a world apart from the traditional opening day rites of spring.

Outdoor magazines and sporting catalogs feature covers with pink-tinted peaks, clear, cold creeks and campfires. More often than not, they depict a pipe-smoking, grandfatherly type imparting the wisdom of stream craft to an attentive adolescent.

Most trout play in pretty places. But the trout water for 5- to 10-year-old kids in the city followed the route of the San Francisco Municipal Railway system's #15 3rd and Kearny bus which deposited you in front of the Cow Palace on Geneva Avenue. Where, each January, the San Francisco Sports and Boat Show came to town, and with it—in a far pavilion—The Huck Finn Pool graciously hosted by the *San Francisco Examiner* and ringmastered by their rod and gun columnist Ed Neal.

A rectangular pond was built with concrete blocks, and a large sky-blue pool liner was recessed over the blocks for effect and practicalness. Above the length of the pool, brass hose nozzles circulated a thunderous stream of spring water. The water was provided by the city's very own Belfast Old Fashion Mug Root Beer Company, whose "spring" was on Evans Avenue. Six-inch rainbow trout were replenished daily from a private hatchery in the Santa Cruz Mountains. To further sweeten the pot, the Shasta Wonderland booth would add lunker trout from their aquarium display.

To fish for free, a youngster would fill out a make believe license that was placed in a chicken wire barrel. A drawing was held every 15 minutes, which was also the length of your angling experience. And some lucky child would return home the proud owner of a new rod and reel.

For 10 days, it appeared as though the entire San Francisco Unified School District, and the parochial schools converged on the pool. The mouse house in Anaheim was not built yet, but those serpentine lines at the pond would equal theirs. When a school buzzer sounded the pond was open for business.

Grandfather and uncle types in the person of members of the Golden Gate Angling and Casting Club, the Pacific Rod and Gun Club, the Tyee Club, and other associated sportsmen organizations personally mentored each child in baiting, casting, and catching a trout or two. The fish were thoughtfully placed in a waxed paper sandwich bag for the trip home.

On the horizon, of about the 4th grade, Lake Merced loomed by the beach with its catchable rainbows and the occasional brook trout planting. Or there was the watercress-choked little Los Lobos Creek in the Presidio with its finger-sized trout fry. And for the more adventurous—the Japanese Tea Garden's pond with trout released from Steinhart Aquarium.

Like a deep first love, that first angling exercise becomes an enduring childhood remembrance. That a fatherless boy, or girl, from a poor part of town could be introduced to the angling arts beside Bing Crosby's threesome as equals, is no small thing.

It conjures up the spirit of Marquez's "Magical Realism," because it was true, all of it.

# Candlestick Point Places

I grew up in a part of San Francisco that has never seen a tour bus. Back then, as now, it was called "The Bayview" and for obvious reasons. The circumference of this small valley was bounded by three hills. The north hill was wide open range, ringed by a few horse stables. The west hill, west of Third Street, was residential homes. And the south hill was a dairy, Christopher Dairy, with black and white Holsteins. The fourth side was bordered by San Francisco Bay.

When I was young, I'd been told that our neighborhood was "famous" for its fine weather. Not Redwood City famous (weather best by government test) but known near and far, mostly near, for fog-free afternoons. Unlike today, this World War II era time was free of federal housing projects and automatic firearms. Italian, Irish, and Maltese Catholic families were common, with a liberal sprinkling of the Orient, the industrious Chinese mercantiling the valley. I can remember my favorite time of month back then was when I collected for my paper route. Door step fragrances emitted aromatic Sicilian fish stews, rich red gravies constituted from salt pork bases laced with pot roast, and those far eastern recipes: plum and mandarin infused dishes that are as much a mystery today as they were back then.

Back around 1915, my grandparents bought eight city lots in the Bayview. They built the family home on one. Later my Uncles and my father were allowed to build homes on three others. The other four lots were reserved for commerce. My grandmother raised and sold chickens, ducks, geese, and fruit on site. There are degrees of toughness: tough, tougher, and toughest. My grandmother was the toughest. Schwarzenegger tough. She could ring the necks of four live chickens, two in each hand, simultaneously. My equally enterprising grandfather constructed a never ending woodshed of scrap lumber and sold salvaged and discarded lumber to equally conservative Italians. A house made of wood was a constant source of wonder for grandfather; there were none in Italy back then, nor today.

We did not live far from "Butchertown"—three city blocks of stockyards and meatpacking plants. Back then, it was quite natural for me to see trainloads, and later truckloads of live cattle, pigs, sheep and goats going through the neighborhood. Occasionally, my grandfather would return home from there with a very small, and very live goat or sheep, and once a pig in the back of his '47 Ford pickup. These animals were never pets. Later on in their very short lives, they would be transformed into various forms of salami and capretto. Years ago I was returning home from Market Street on a city bus. The traffic on Third was stopped. From my Muni bus seat, I watched three wild-eyed steers run past my window seat with horse and cowboy in hot pursuit. The cowboy was waving a lariat rope over his head, just like in the movies. A stockyard fence had collapsed.

Strange as it may seem, up through the '40s, the '50s and into the early '60s, nearly everyone we knew spoke Italian. Except for the Chinese. It was then that we would use English as a second language to communicate. My grandparents would never learn to speak English. Italian merchants ran the banks (Bank of Italy later reconfigured to the Bank of America), the markets, the produce stands, the bakeries, and most importantly, the local creamery, the home of homemade ice cream, burgers and hotdogs that our fast-food nation children would never understand. My grandfather used to say that our whole block was Italian until 1947. That's when "The American" (La Americano) moved in. He was from Oklahoma and worked at a shipyard nearby. My grandfather marveled at the American as though he was from outer space. By 1950, the American was drinking my grandfather's unfiltered, unirrigated, unsulfited, zinfandel like water and yelling like a local, in Italian.

It seems only logical, to me, that many Italians would relocate and feel familiar with San Francisco. The two, Italy and San Francisco, are surrounded by big blue water and seafood. The Bay began just east of my grandmother's tomatoes. Just south of there, at the foot of Gilman Avenue, a promontory stretched out into the Bay, with a distinctive twelve foot high rock at its very end. At low tide, this grey-black-green rock, incongruently standing alone on a white shell beach, was analogized as a slightly tilting candlestick and base. It was called "the candlestick."

The alchemy in my childhood was at the base of that rock—the tide pools. Water elevated, receded, and revealed something new nearly every day. My first favorites were the dime-sized Dungeness crabs, easily transportable in a mayonnaise jar. I can recall transporting a few home and looking forward to a long-lasting pet-friend relationship, like Lassie and Timmy on TV. The crabs lasted for a day; maybe a day and a half. I looked at my non-future friends, claws up at the bottom of the jar, and realized early on that frogs, butterflies and caterpillars were best left alone in their natural habitat.

Still, like that moth and that flame, I was drawn back to those pools. On the bottom of the big pools were cantankerous old bullheads. With their shades of dark brown and black, and with small horns on their heads, they reminded me of mean old people who didn't want to be bothered by anyone. I always obliged them. There was a small green perch that we called a "pogie" that made a regular appearance. A silver-sided fish, palm-sized, that we called "shiners" rose recklessly to shrimp baited hooks like piranha. Every now and then blue-backed anchovies with their gaping mouths showed up and were retrieved by my father. The anchovies were brought home, fried in olive oil, and were usually a complement to black-shelled bay mussels. A stray smelt was always dismissed as "having worms." Where that came from is anybody's guess. It must have been an Italian taboo as I recall going over to Hunters Point with my parents to buy boiled shrimp from the Chinese commercial fisherman, peering into their pots, and noting the skeletal remains of smelt. By the way, they looked, and smelled good to me.

There was this guy on our block by the name of Joe San Falippo, a Sicilian. Folks would call him "Josan" in one word, like it was his name. Josan would appear on the beach near the candlestick for the first southeaster of the season. A southeaster is a particularly powerful winter storm that blows up from that direction. From a second story window we would watch Josan in the wind, water, and rain reaching into the foam for white shell sea snails that had broken free from their deep Bay beds. He loaded galvanized buckets full. Once I was honored with a bowl of his sea snail stew that I can still taste. Should you be going northbound towards the city on #101, look over towards the Candlestick Park offramp and observe a white shell beach; they're sea snail shells.

Back then, it was customary to fish Candlestick Point for striped bass with bait. The Del Monte folks were still canning the soon-to-be-ghost sardines at the end of Pier 90. The good sardines were placed in rounds and tins of tomato paste and olive oil a la Italiani. The bad sardines wound up at the local bait shops. The sardines were sold in a shoebox, three to a pound, packed on ice and covered with sawdust. The box was wrapped in newspaper and secured with twine. A box sold for fifty cents and was designed to last four hours; the last two and first two hours of the incoming and outgoing tide. On the blue moon rare occasions that my family hooked and landed a striper, it graced our Sunday afternoon family suppers. The oven baked bass was immersed in an ocean of tomato sauce and garnished with the usual suspects: potatoes, peas, and carrots. I can never ever remember there being great jubilation amongst my sisters and brother when this fish appeared as table fare.

The year 1950 saw the eighth wonder of the world appear in the form of two aluminum boats that were purchased from my father's uncle in Marin County. His uncle began building boats in San Rafael, off Canal

Street. The company was called Trailorboats. The most famous model was the Klamath. It was a doozey. The Pacific Gas and Electric Company thought enough of them to use them as ice breakers on frozen Sierra lakes. By way of a pair of ten-horse Elgin's, my uncles Guido and Giovanni, and my father Alfredo became "trollers." And to hear to the three of them talk back then, they were "experts" to anyone that would listen. They used a Tony Accetta chrome pet spoon or a white bug eye jig, depending on the tide. The lures were tipped with a hooked pork rind trailer. Back then, these lures were deadly at Candlestick, and if you could find them, they probably still are. Those three (and later me) caught lots of bass. Lots of 'em.

In 1957 the New York Giants baseball club came to town. One year later a local contractor by the name of George Harney brought earth moving equipment to the top of the Bayview's south hill. I watched that gang sheer the top off that hill and push it into the Bay for a new ballpark. If my bearings are right, and I think they are, the candlestick rock is forever memorialized beneath the western most part of the section "H" parking lot.

Oddly enough, the Bay fill had no effect on the stripers. Every summer and fall the stripers appeared throughout the '60s. Not big ones, they never were; "schoolies" we called them. We started using flies for fun. Big fun. Doug Merrick and I fished through the '70s and late '80s with the same results.

Tom Chin and I fished there last month, and the fish were still there—lots of 'em.

# Stocking San Francisco

I grew up near McLaren Park in the southeast corner of the city. McLaren Park had nothing to do with being a park. It was "open space," before the term was coined. If you were looking for a wooded area, say a small forest with an enchantress and a happy gnome or two, this was not your place. This park was famous for body drops, stripping cars, and mayhem. In my age group there was a crew of 12-year-old Italian kids who were practicing for the future. They were promising young hoodlums, and when I look back at it, they were somewhat ethical. "Lucky" was the leader, and "Fast Eddie" was the enforcer. For instance, if you were "jumped" by these junior racketeers you were merely robbed by force or fear, and if you had no money you were "jacked up." They gave you options too, using sign language; a raised right fist meant the hospital, a left, the morgue. If dog walking was your thing, an attack trained poodle would be hopeless against those hooligans, a meat eating Doberman would have to do. Lacking man's best friend, you'd be wise to "pack heat" on a walkabout. Most kids growing up played, explored, or climbed trees in their local parks. I ran for my life and climbed trees for survival. One time when I had received a particularly thorough thrashing from those choir boys, Lucky told me not to take this whipping "personal" it was "just business." I understood.

As you can imagine, our neighborhood was made up of blue collar Italian immigrants with little money. There were no social events like a Friday night fish fry at the Elks, Moose, Lions or any other "animal" lodges because there were no lodges. For the most part, people worked hard all week, and on weekends they drank wine, ate macaroni, played guitars and sang like Caruso when prompted.

Obviously this was before the world was a one-click-window. The world then was black and white, like TV. For instance, June Cleaver was on the tube wearing high heels and pearls as she made a meatloaf. Upstairs, Eddie Haskell, a friend of the Beaver's older brother was methodically dismembering the Beaver. The young mobsters at the park were big fans of the "Untouchables," an Al Capone gangland weekly. At the movies, either way out west, or to the shores of Tripoli, you could always count on John Wayne for a 90-minute fistfight. So you see, it wasn't just our neighborhood with all these problems. There was just violence in the air, everywhere.

One spring, in the '60s, the City and County of San Francisco participated in a federally funded grant entitled "Urban Renewal." I am certain my section of the city qualified first. They paved a road through the park and even built a reservoir with a parking lot above it. There was a sign that directed people to what they called "The Duck Pond," and this was always a major mystery to us kids. No green headed mallards were ever noted, no bull sprig taking wing, just mud hens and a thing we called a "Goony Bird," cackling constantly. The pond was love at first sight for the locals though. Nearly every night the overlook became a lover's lane, winos held conventions up there, and car thieves rolled car carcasses down the hill and into the pond bottom. During the day we kids rode our bikes around the reservoir, over, through and around undergarments, beer bottles, and car rear ends.

One of my bike paisanos was a kid we called "Joey Bagadonuts." His real name was Joey Bachagalupi of course, and we called him "Joeybags" for short. At school reunions classmates often speak of having gone through 12 years of schooling. Joey spent 13. One year his term ending report card had this notation from a nun, "Not to advance to the next level." Joey saw a silver lining in flunking the 6th grade. It meant an extra year patrolling the hallways ensconced in the heady fragrance of lockers filled with lunch bags loaded with tuna fish and bananas. It was his favorite class between classes.

One day when we were in the 8ᵗʰ grade, Joey told us he was going to work a summer job at the Steinhart Aquarium in San Francisco's Golden Gate Park. He was going to be an assistant to his Uncle Primo, who he said was a "scientist" at the aquarium. From what I knew about Joey, there was nothing in his family and his background suggesting scholastic achievement. Joey said it was no big deal to him, and it wasn't. It turns out Primo and his "assistant scientist" scrubbed and scraped the lifeless aquarium tanks free of algae and scum, and removed dead or dying fish to the galvanized garbage cans in the back of the aquarium.

One summer evening Joey told me about the those luckless living fish in the back of the aquarium that had done their job and been drummed out of "show business" for new acts. We thought it over. There were gonna be no more dark days in the aquarium, or garbage cans for these fish. We were going to give them some blue sky.

We'd stock our lake in San Francisco with fish.

Late one Sunday afternoon my brother Will and I, in his '53 Dodge pickup, went to the rear of the aquarium and waited until hardly anyone was around. The rendezvous with Joey took place without incident. Quickly, we removed two cans of tropical looking fish and three turtles, and drove up to the lake. It's safe to say the fish were not what I had in mind. They were as colorful as an old stamp collection and yet a small harbinger of things to come. We took solace in the fact that there was not a piranha in the bunch. We think.

Joey was gonna have to do some reconnaissance work. We wanted something bigger than goldfish. Two weeks later we hit the big bonanza. Joey called and said the aquarium was going to dispose of the contents of one tank, "The California Coast," an exhibition of freshwater shrimp, a dozen small Steelhead trout, three or four grilse salmon, a four foot sturgeon, and 200 to 300 striped bass fingerlings.

11

Eureka!

Towards twilight we were headed up the hill with three garbage cans of fish. When we arrived, the turtles were resting comfortably on the roof of a submerged Mercury looking at nothing in particular. All the fish hit the drink without incident except the sturgeon. He was pissed off. He whiplashed my brother on the side of his head with his tail. Later, Will said he saw Tinkerbelle in orbit around his head when he was whirling towards terra firma.

That evening we sat on the hood of my brother's pickup in the parking lot looking down on the pond's surface. Concentric circles spun on its surface in the fading light.

The next morning was still, as it always is in the city. We rode our bikes up to the lake and watched while small schools of fish paralleled the shoreline, some leaped, others rolled, and the two turtles took it all in from the hardtop roof.

Neither Joey nor I expected anything, or knew what we had accomplished. It was simply just a good thing. Letting some living creature live was enough for us. That's not to say that we did not catch a few on spinners because we did, but we always released them. What would be the point otherwise?

Well they swam and they swam all over the damn summer. The winos watched in rapture. The lovers up on the lane watched the parade swim by and the car thieves continued to recycle and discard parts in the pond. Not surprisingly, there were fewer evening rises, and less fish as that summer progressed. As word reached the neighborhood, the low ethical standards continued. They were keeping the fish.

A lake is no longer a novelty when there is nothing left. We moved on.

Tail winds and time saw me through high school and the service, and now and again I would recall the memory of it all, that summer when wild fish rose to a dry fly within the city limits of San Francisco.

While I was away fighting imagined enemies in a war that America did not believe in, my blessed mother would often send me a care package of sorts. It always included interesting snippets clipped from the *Chronicle* or the *Examiner*. One entry was a touchstone. The pond had been drained and a sturgeon and several striped bass were living well. They were released into the Bay.

On my last trip into the city I took a trip up to the lake to look things over. On the way I thought of Lucky and Fast Eddie. For sure they were not at the park singing "That old gang of mine" like some barbershop quartet. I'd heard years earlier that Lucky had been in jail, and Fast Eddie was bankrupt and living alone.

The lake was still there though. Two chain link fences, with holes you could drive an SUV through, circled the pond. Debris, broken glass, and an oil slick adhering to the pond's windward shore were strong evidence that the grandchildren of the goons who gave me hell years ago were still at play, and that up and coming car thieves were busy working their way towards a future filled with lock downs and orange jump suits.

Driving west out through the park I was struck by a sign directing me to the Jerry Garcia Amphitheater. Then I remembered someone somewhere saying that he had lived near the park when he was young. Reaching back in my mind I cannot recollect anyone contemplatively strumming a six string in this park, and yet, I can easily visualize a guitar totting kid "truckin" rapidly towards safety with hard-charging hooligans in pursuit. One more thing, and this is the last thing: That "long strange trip" that he and his Grateful Dead bandmates sang about, I wonder, was he thinking about McLaren Park?

13

# Islais Creek & The Coot

ISLAIS CREEK

1. Islais (is-lay-is) Muwekema (California Coastal Indian Tribe) word for the holly leaf cherry.

2. A historic three-mile-long freshwater creek that began on the south flank of Twin Peaks in San Francisco. The creek occupied a 5000 acre watershed. Its springs and tributaries supplied 85% of San Francisco's drinking water in the early 1800s. The creek flowed southeast, joined Cayuga Creek near Mission Street and flowed southeasterly into San Francisco Bay. There were abundant fish and wildlife in its marshes and estuary. Shrimp, herring and silver smelt spawned in its waterways. Mussels, crabs, and crustaceans oozed prolifically on its tidal flats. Great barges from California's Central Valley unloaded their hay and grain on its protected waters.

SF City & County Publication
San Francisco Public Library
Main Branch
1949

COOT

1. *Fulica americana.* A North American water bird; slate grey, plump, with a white beak. Looks like a duck, acts like a duck, is not a duck. Lazy, it flies only under duress, and not very well—certainly not very high or far. Unable to navigate very well in water. Thrashes about with little or no forward progress. Uncommonly large feet impede this bird's walkabouts on land. Heartbreakingly homely in appearance, it is commonly referred to as the "mud hen."

Wingspans over the West
1961

15

The Islais Creek that our red brothers foraged and fished on bears no resemblance to today's model. Over the last 150 years the creek has been chopped, channeled, concreted and covered. Old timers can recall the upper creek basin as having the largest sardine factory on the globe, and livestock being delivered to "Butchertown" on the creek's banks. Tramp steamers returning from the South Seas lined the wharfs. Conveyer belts with large metal buckets dug deep into the holds of these ships, unloading coconuts and bananas. Fruit fragrances filled the air.

In the 1960s, containerized cargo cranked up in Oakland and swallowed San Francisco's seaport industry. The creek lived on as a storm drain release, and as the city's sewer outfall. When wooden fishing boats worked Bay waters they would moor beside the sewer plant. The sewer effluent eradicated seaweed growth and barnacles on boat bottoms, as well as eradicating nearly every living organism in the creek's ecosystem. San Franciscans privately, not publicly, referred to the creek by its nickname, "s- -t creek."

Years ago, on the Bay at Mission Basin, the remains of an unseaworthy wooden ship weighed anchor. The boat had no business being afloat. It had been ravaged by weather, time, and theft. The boat had been rendered rudderless, engineless and, through preplanning and piracy, had its pilot house removed in broad daylight. It rested just off shore from San Francisco Marine, a machine shop that catered to the maritime industry.

Back in the early 1950s, Tino was our next-door neighbor. Like every Italian I ever met, and according to him, he was an expert at everything: construction, cooking, a Casanova (3+ wives), a winemaker, an artist, an accordion player, and according to him, a "man of respect." He worked on the waterfront his whole life. Tino was a living legend down on the docks. Among his other talents he was a top-drawer fisherman, a first-class moocher, and a thief. After WWII he went to work as longshoreman, a highly lucrative way of life on the waterfront before containerization. In less than a year's time he went from his businessman's coupe to a 1950 Ford pickup to haul "his stuff" home. When they put the locks on the docks, Tino went to work for San Francisco Marine. Their parts department was right up his alley.

The San Francisco Maritime Museum had nothing on Tino's garage. He had more manila hemp rope than the Philippine Islands could manufacture in a decade. His buddies, the stevedores, were always surprised when they were in his basement—surprised that there was any line left to tie ships to the wharfs. He had unopened 60-gallon barrels of unknown origins and contents lined against the walls. An Eskimo canoe hung from his rafters, and from time to time exotic birds in cages appeared. Two small black-spotted South American leopards called ocelots showed up at his home. Marlin Perkins' "Wild Kingdom" came to mind. Oddly enough, Tino never sold the things he stole. He collected them. I suspect he wanted to keep in touch with his craft in case hard times hit.

Back to the boat. One morning the boat beside the marine shop vanished and reappeared up the creek and among the fishing fleet. Tino stole it. Jean Lafitte, the pirate, and Al Capone's blood lay latent in his ancestry. Tino christened his craft "The Coot" in honor of the ugly duckling.

The keel for the Coot was laid in 1926. It was built along the lines of the Bismarck, a German battleship, turtle slow, uncommonly heavy, and just plain hard to envision at sea. Retrofitting the Coot was easily arranged. A Cummings marine diesel, a brass rudder, and the personnel property of who knows who from God knows where. The Coot was ready to set sail in very short order. And sail she did. When underway in rough water there was no pitch, no yawl, no unsteady swaying. She could have been the first cousin of a Coast Guard cutter.

Tino was entrepreneurial in that he always combined business with pleasure. When he went fishing, he always sold the fish. He always took his neighbors, family and friends fishing. We paid for gas, lunch, and your catch was his to keep so that he could "make expenses." I caught and lost my first striped bass to "expenses." My first King salmon went south the very same way, and come to think of it, my first silver salmon too. Oddly enough though, it didn't seem to matter. Wide open water and sea breezes seemed reward enough.

When we were ocean fishing on the Coot one summer, my uncle Guido caught a big fish near Point Lobos. We brought it back to Muni Bait in the Marina to weigh it and find out what it was. It was a California White Seabass, and it became bouillabaisse at a French restaurant by nightfall. Logical anglers always cut their lines when a stingray was hooked. The old Dagos would speak of an electrical shock which could place you in a coma if you were stung by a ray. Tino always flipped the rays upside down and scooped their white wings out, making "scallops" for Cioppino Zuppa, a house specialty down on the wharfs. Another time Tony, a friend of mine, and some friends were playing down on the rocks at Gilman Beach, which was a beach before they put Candlestick Park on top of it. A 290-pound 7-gill Lemon Shark chased him out of the water. The shark lodged itself between two rocks, and the boys let him have it with rocks. They were Italian kids, they knew all about revenge. Several fisherman brought the shark to Slims Bait Shop on 3rd Street. The papers came to take pictures of Tony and the shark. Later that day, Steinhart Aquarium called and requested the shark for scientific study. It was the second largest ever recorded at that time. Way too late. It was already in the back of Tino's truck on its way to "I Hope So," a restaurant in Chinatown.

Tino liked to fish at night, when it is illegal to do so. Stripers were his specialty. The Coot would come out of the creek around 3:00 a.m., boat running lights off, and shoot straight past those marvelous Matson Ocean Liners, the *Lurline*, the *Matsonia*, the *Mariposa* (locals called them the "hula ships"), and on up to the Richmond San Rafael Bridge. The bridge lights on the San Rafael side were low and very luminous. Even today, those lights can still make Broadway, the Great White Way, blush. The lights attract a blitzkrieg of baitfish, bass, and always, illegal anglers. Tino and his gang would load up with a legal limit (he had ethics), lift anchor, and head home.

Tino was taken away a long time ago to the state hospital in Napa where people do not know their own names.

Down on the creek, the California chorus frog croaks in the pickleweed, and discarded old fishing boats fluctuate with the tide. The appearance is that of an ancient elephant burial ground where boats go when it's time to leave their life. The Coot is among them.

Some say that the sound of anchor chains are a ship's way of communicating with each other. Lets hope so, the Coot has a lot to say.

# Up the River

In each and every one of us there is at least one ribbon of running water that flows through our very being.

If you were born in Rome, you would mention the Tiber. Paris? The Seine. Or in London? The Thames.

Around here, we could never count on the Sacramento or the San Joaquin Rivers as our own. Others might say that the San Lorenzo, down Santa Cruz way, could be all things to all people. Maybe, but probably not.

A San Franciscan would say it could only be the Russian River, 60 miles north of the Golden Gate toll plaza. It was, and still is, our home recreational river for all seasons and reasons.

A local exchanging pleasantries with another during the summer season poses a question, "Where you going this weekend?" "Up the river," would be the response. Or, "Hey, where's Joe at?" And another "Up the river" reply. This was, and still is, a common colloquialism around these parts.

After the construction of Mendocino Dam in Ukiah, and certainly after Warm Springs Dam in Sonoma, the Russian became a rapidless river. In earlier times before the dams, that stream socked it to us every winter. Every newspaper, and we had lots of them back then, had photographs of people on their rooftops waving their hands towards the heavens as rescuing helicopters hovered above, or of a guy in a motorboat flying full bore down Guerneville's main drag with a couch, a TV or a dog on the front seat headed toward higher ground. In those days, the TV and radio stations issued flood stage reports as commonly as the stock report.

Back in 1953, my Uncle Guido and my father Alfredo built a summer home in Armstrong Woods, five miles east of the river on what the realtor described as a "high bench" that had never flooded. In 1955 all hell broke loose. Thunder, lightning and rain eclipsed all records. Noah's deal was nothing, and the summer cabin became an unrecognizable calamity. Apparently San Franciscans back then had short memories too. Everyone rebuilt their homes in 1956, and kept them, or looked for an unsuspecting buyer.

In the spring, when the water went back to the riverbed where it was supposed to be, we started to fish for shad. I'd like to say that I caught lots and lots of them, but I didn't. I was usually in elementary school. Shad weren't much fun anyway, and they imparted an unusual odor. I could usually catch a trout/salmon or steelhead smolts in Armstrong Creek, in the redwoods. Even back then I was into aesthetics.

In late spring, the cabin crowd went "up the river" to work and get things ready for summer. I was a "big picture" kind of guy. I went down to the river and fished for smallmouth bass on spinners. Spin fishing was huge back then. It made experts out of ordinary guys, like me. No backwater, cove, or overhang was out of the question from the opposite bank, flip the reel bail and let it fly!

One summer during my Boy Scout years, when I had just turned 11, my parents sent my brother and me off to Camp Royaneh, near Cazadero, on Austin Creek, a small tributary to the Russian River. It's near the ocean, and that forever fog that the California coastline is famous for. We slept in canvas tents, beneath redwood trees that dripped dew on us all night long.

The drumbeat and flag flying at scout camp began each morning at 6 a.m. with a real cannon blast across Austin Creek. Then it was "up and at 'em" towards the mess hall, my first encounter with powdered eggs for breakfast. This "wildness" or wilderness-ness of scouting truly perplexed me for one particular reason. Less than 4 miles south of our campsites the Italian dinner houses in Occidental were imparting the full fragrance of their gravies simmering into the early morning air. I come from a family of heavy eaters. I cannot recall my stomach ever growling. People my size think that "We better get something to eat" or "just in case" all day long. A pancake, powdered eggs, and milk seemed to be a sad substitute to chicken cacciatore, a bowl of pasta asciutto, and powdered apple fritters just over the ridgeline.

The saving grace of Royaneh (some sort of Indian word for group or tribe somewhere) was Austin Creek, its canoes and fish. The stream was a staircase of small dams and I aimed to explore them all, and did, as far down as its confluence with the Russian, maybe 400 feet away.

Plenty of scouts were into horseback riding, basket weaving, pottery, the merit badge thing. I came to camp with what we called "frogman" gear: a snorkel, fins, and a face mask. It's easy to explain. It was the early days of television and one program featured an actor named Lloyd Bridges as an action hero frogman going up and down southern California coast saving blondes, busting up crime, and defusing bombs. I was deeply influenced.

My automatic angling method was really simple, and even this late in life I reminisce about its genius. Snorkel during the day, look over the creekscape, and raise hell near nightfall with a super duper at pre-selected sites. It's safe to say that the super duper was my favorite lure back then. The packaging said the lures motion imparted a "crippled minnow action" that drove fish nuts. I caught the same 4 and 5 inch rainbows over and over. Some were spun silly by the lure's action, making confused circles when released, until they straightened themselves out. I recollect curious, crazy-looking crawdads coming up from the depths to check out the action, or positioning themselves for a fish feast. Most of these trout were lucky enough make it out to sea, while others were cannibalized by smallmouth at the confluence. On occasion, I could catch a glimpse of large carp or catfish. You would need some sort of stink bait to catch them. I had standards. I was into luring my prey. After all, and mobsters aside, we Italians are all about self respect.

On warm summer Saturday nights, just up river from Guerneville, there was a teen dance in the open air auditorium at Monte Rio. Every high school in the city was represented, Catholic, public, and trade schools. They used to have what was called "The Battle of the Bands," with lots of dancing and romancing all around. More often then not, another "battle" took place that had nothing to do with the bands. The rough and rowdy guys from each school met for a bit of "knuckle city action" between schools. I was way too young for the rough stuff or romance. While the music from the dance hall serenaded the summer sky, my friends and I slipped up, over and around the summer dams on "borrowed" canoes, casting like mad men by the light of the silvery moon.

September's song was always the same. Just as Labor Day concluded we San Franciscans pulled the shade on the whole river scene. We would "button up" the cabins for the winter, just like that. Late summer? Forget it. Indian summer? Not a chance. Fall? Nonexistent. Unless of course you were a fisherman.

By late October any shopkeeper along the river with any sense at all had shuttered up for the winter. Guerneville's Grant King, at King's Sport & Tackle did the opposite. He was stocking his shelves with all kinds of gizmos and gadgets that attracted fish, as well as fishermen from all over.

The silver salmon would be breeching the sandbar at Jenner soon. If the rains came late, a local fisherman/farmer would lend a hand with his D5 Caterpillar and carve a causeway from the river to the surf line to allow the early silvers to slide through. This little tractor was nicknamed "Mighty Mouse" for its small size and strength.

In December, all anglers looked for a light rain to raise this green river to a light grey and recede back to a grey-green. Think steelhead. We took to this watershed in well-established, and time-honored configurations. Generally, the Ukiah crowd hung tough at the most northerly section: the east fork of the Russian, Pieta Creek and Squaw Rock. The central section of the river, Healdsburg, was inhabited by the Santa Rosa gang, the city slickers clung to the lower reaches, down to the river's running end, the estuary that began just east of Monte Rio.

King's Sport & Tackle (and flies) anchored all fishing events in the area, dispensing tackle, tips, and holding a steelhead contest. Storefront fish photos changed daily, as frequently as did the first place fish. Someone somewhere on the river seemed to place nationally in the annual *Field & Stream* Fishing contest. The Russian would always weigh in with a 22- to 24-pounder, automatically.

This is off the subject but I am gonna tack it on anyway. On the west side of King's was Pat's coffee shop. For years there was a hand painted signed that read "hot cakes." When I walked to the river in the winter to fish I'd walk by the coffee shop and conjure up images of a hot cake. Were they different flavors? Like chocolate? Vanilla? At 12, paper route money was in full flow. I went in and ordered a "hot cake" like I knew what I was talking about. I was served a single pancake.

Somewhere short of the seventies, the gene pool of the big bruiser steelhead perished. Certainly the two dams altered spawning habitat on the Russian. Vineyard development, coupled with commercial and residential needs from Santa Rosa to southern Marin, also changed the river. Lastly, there were no seals to speak of then. Now at least ninety wait patiently at Jenner for anything silver passing through this gauntlet. Back in the day, when we won our last World War, sea captains, party boat skippers, and the commercial boys dealt with fish-snatching seals in a new and nonlethal way. Please remember that the time I speak of was 60 years ago, just after the last real war we won. A flare gun blast to the arse put those seals on edge and running for cover.

The Department of Fish and Game learned a lesson from a ladderless Mendocino Dam. A hatchery was constructed below Warm Springs Dam on Dry Creek. The eggs of returning steelhead are incubated on site, and subsequently released 14 months later, 35 miles upstream at the base of the Mendocino Dam. The fish are usually released on a spring river swelling, and the added distance upstream aids olfactory development.

Best of all, the returning steelhead are first cousins of the historical runs. Native strains were removed from the headwaters of Dry Creek above Lake Sonoma and nurtured to a self-sustaining level. About ten thousand steelhead yearlings are released, and between two thousand and twenty-five hundred make it back each year.

Well, I guess that's about all I can recollect about this river, except to say: What a river it is.

# Dan Bailey's Vest

It was a time long ago, before that river ran over and through us. Lets say the early 1950s, when America was awfully strong and made car bumpers heavier than some of today's models. Vehicles had not sprouted those fins yet either.

On his 8th birthday he received a Mitchell 300 spinning reel and a Shakespeare rod from a rich uncle. His father took him down to Barry's Army-Navy Surplus Store, off Mission Street in San Francisco and bought him an old gas mask satchel that hung down to his knees. That was his "creel" so to speak. Most of his friends had official tackle boxes, civilized stuff.

The San Francisco Municipal Railway system transported his older brother, him, and the gas mask bag overland towards exotic (to him) locations—the Municipal Pier in North Beach for instance. A nickel's worth of prawns (3-5) from the Muni Bait Shop put him in business. Lake Merced, three long bus transfers from home, was a serious commitment. Those trout reeled him in nearly every weekend. He particularly liked "The Sugar House" on 3rd Street beneath Potrero Hill. Claus Spreckles had built an eleven-story sugar refinery. It was constructed of six million red bricks. Pumps delivered 8000 gallons per minute of water from the Bay to cool the machinery. The fish truly enjoyed the warm water discharge. Lots of them spent the winter there. The magic of moving water, the discharge, was the first semi-river he had ever fished.

The 11th summer of his life took him to Alpine County, south of Lake Tahoe, on a camping trip to a genuine trout stream in the form of Markleeville Creek. One morning he watched a fisherman in hip boots, wearing a vest and carrying a fly rod, swing through the campground and up the creek. He was watching an "expert." All fly fishermen were experts back then, and they looked it, he thought.

A full turn of the calendar later, an uncle and his spouse drove to Montana—a trip he and she would repeat yearly, until they both walked off the earth into the night. His city-born-and-bred uncle returned "full western," wearing a John B. Stetson hat, a hubcap-sized belt buckle, with a fly rod, reel and fishing vest from Dan Bailey's Fly Shop in Livingston, Montana. In the blink of a season his uncle had become a "fly fisherman."

San Pedro Valley Creek flows west out of the Coast Range three miles south of San Francisco. His uncle took him fishing there. They caught scrappy six-inch rainbows. His uncle used a royal coachman fly, a Christmas tree looking pattern. He used salmon eggs, and sensed that he was feeling the lure of this fly fishing. He sent for a Dan Bailey catalog. At age 12, he had the fever. Bad.

He bought a Wright and McGill fly rod, an imitation Hardy Heddon fly reel, and a level fly line. The gas mask bag was still *de rigueur* as he did not know how to order, size up, or buy a vest.

In January, most men are looking forward to the Super Bowl, or baseball's spring training. He looked forward to the Dan Bailey Fly Shop catalog. He read and studied it like a scholar analyzing the Dead Sea Scrolls.

Like a moth to a flame, he continually returned to the fishing vest section. One in particular made his eyebrows rise up to the top of his forehead in amazement: "The Vest" by Dan Bailey. Dan Bailey, an expert fisherman, professional fishermen, and outdoor writers concluded it was the best trout vest ever produced for the serious fisherman. His hair stood on end when he read that "The Vest" was inspired, born, and tested on the banks of the Yellowstone River, and that this super-tough polyester/cotton fabric prototype withstood 2,400 hours of field use without "a dent." The advertisement continued on that the services of Stan Hui, a high fashion Hong Kong tailor (ourhi kh ltd.) had been hired to handcraft each vest. That did it, he'd swallowed the ad's pitch, hook, line and sinker.

It would take three solid months of paper route money to obtain the vest. Easily arranged he thought. Among other things, daydreaming was his hobby. It was easy for him to imagine each newspaper tossed was a long and very accurate cast to a particularly difficult fish lie, and in his mind it was no big deal because he was a fly fisherman, an expert.

Winter was concluding when the vest arrived. He opened the box slowly, like an archeologist exhuming King Tut's tomb. Reverently, he held up the two-tone brown vest and put it on. Back then, the trout season in California opened on the closest Saturday to May 1st. He imagined that spring day as a member of the opening day fraternity, a fly fisherman, no less.

The story of where the vest went, or with whom, takes on a life of its own. It was passed onto the shoulders of his youngest son years ago. And this spring, with the birth of his son's son, the vest will be passed on again.

It's safe to say that an angling accoutrement is not quite like, or as sentimental as, that first kiss, or that first love. Yet it does have meaning, like a long life, or hope. Pass it on.

# An Old San Francisco Saying

*"Shake the Hand that Shook the Hand"*

It's been said that a man's handshake is measured in terms of congeniality, commitment, and kindness. True enough, and never truer than in San Francisco.

Back in the '30s, my uncle Andy was more than an acquaintance of Lefty O'Doul, a major league baseball player and a native San Franciscan. Lefty grew up in the Bayview district of the city at a time when the Italians were moving out of North Beach to the southeast corner of the city and finding open space. "*La Campagna*," the country, they called it.

Lefty still sports the 4th highest batting average of all time, .348, and in 1939 he batted .398. Andy mentioned that Lefty returned to his roots yearly by visiting Burnett Elementary school and dispensing miniature wooden bats to young Andy and his classmates. At that time, Lefty was the toast of New York, the National League, and Burnett Elementary School. Baseball back then, as now, was a very big deal.

Along 3rd Street in smoky old saloons there was a somewhat customary greeting as a wag entered, "Boys shake the hand that shook the hand of Lefty O'Doul!" To anyone listening, it was meant to impart a high social standing, great status, and with any luck at all, a free drink from the 80-proofers present.

Andy was an "athalete." That's how it was annunciated back then. He was one of the very first to attain "All City" awards in all three sports. He was also a sandlot teammate and lifelong friend of Joe DiMaggio.

My blessed mother once told me that Joe and Reno Barsocchini visited Andy at their house on Gilman Avenue. Andy had injured his ankle in a baseball game. The first visit was based on their friendship, the second and third visits were timed to the tune of my grandmother's pasta asciutta.

Later on in life Joe told me that Andy had hurt himself sliding into second at Father Flanagan's Field on Harrison Street. Joe said it was one of his favorite fields of all time. It had something to do with west winds helping hitters like himself. These days that field takes the form of a big grey tombstone called the Hall of Justice.

One time, Reno made mention of a short trip that the three had taken together. One early morning in the '50s, they went pheasant hunting outside of Antioch. The hunt was successful and concluded early. It was decided that they would grab a quick bite to eat at a Portuguese restaurant in Antioch. Andy carefully covered the guns and birds with a canvas tarp in the back of his pickup truck. The restaurant owner took it upon himself to call friends, and these friends called their friends. They emerged from the restaurant out into a late-afternoon sun. Apparently fans back then were into collectables. The birds, guns, tarp, and a spare tire had been removed as souvenirs.

The first time I met Joe was at the Cow Palace. He and Andy were playing in a celebrity softball game for the KSFO All Stars. Andy introduced me to Joe. Joe reached out and shook my hand and said he was glad to meet me, like I was somehow important. His handshake was long, strong and at the same time gentle. He smiled and looked me right in my eyes, like I meant something memorable. Oddly enough, I had no idea who he was. I was a little kid then. Donald

Duck and that Disney gang would have meant more. Years later though, when we would meet and greet one another and he looked me straight in the eye I somehow felt that by some sort of Andy osmosis I had been an important part of his life, helping him with his record breaking batting streak, his outfielder grace, and then again, I hadn't even been born when he played.

Incidentally, there was no more mention of Lefty in those days. Lefty had been left out of the picture. The choir boys who inhabited the city's watering holes were onto a new slogan "Shake the hand that shook the hand of the Yankee Clipper!" and with it came all the same rights, respect, and privileges that were bestowed on Old Lefty's calling card.

The last time I saw Joe we were at Candlestick Park at a Giants game. We were in a sky box with his granddaughter and her friend. Joe was signing baseballs (American League only) and tossing them to the crowd below. It was part of a promotion for a playing card company. The sky box had a television, a radio, and a waitress who provided any sort of cuisine or libation you wanted on request. Joe liked hotdogs, nachos, and cola.

I was busy watching Joe watch the game. He observed each pitch the pitchers pitched and indicated what type of pitch had been released. More amazing, he could call the pitch inside, outside, high or low and reconfirm his comment by turning around in his chair and watching the replay. He paid no attention to any umpire action. He didn't need to.

The game concluded and we shook hands for what would be my last time. On the way home that day I can recall thinking back to how Joe might have rolled his hands into a high hard one, or caressed one of the most desirable divas ever.

At the funeral home, the night of my uncle Andy's rosary, there were large cardboard sheets on easels. There were photos and clippings of his life and times. I focused on a particularly large photograph taken in Golden Park at the Big Rec baseball diamond. The photo was from the "Sporting Green" of the *San Francisco Chronicle* in 1948. Fans in the grandstand were all attired in white shirts, ties and hats. Out on the playing field the participants were likewise attired and wearing baseball caps.

The pitcher and the batter, in suspenders and tie, were of another place, another time, and in their prime. Andy had just delivered a pitch to Joe, who had swung and missed.

# The Year of the Fortune Cookie

From a very early age he was passionate about parades. His first recollection was of the parade on Columbus Avenue in San Francisco, in 1952. The locals were wearing "I like Ike" buttons and waving red, white and blue flags while a man who would be the future president sped by at 55 mph. His favorite though, had been the Barnum & Bailey Circus parade. Boxcars chock full of God's creatures and critters disembarked at the 3rd Street train yard and proceeded pell-mell up Geneva Avenue and on into the Cow Palace for a week's worth of hijinks.

Crossing Columbus Avenue in the city from North Beach (Little Italy) into Chinatown is a quick cultural exchange. Roman restaurants on one side, and on the other side, bing bong and you're in Hong Kong. As was his yearly custom, he drove into Chinatown to dine, dance, and catch the conclusion of the Chinese Lunar New Year Parade.

The jalopy he drove had been stalling at traffic signals lately, but not tonight—he was armed with a new "DieHard" battery. The rest of the car still looked like hell, and one look at it would automatically have told you that it was useless for anything, particularly for any kind of criminal activity. No self respecting wheel man anywhere would want any part of it for a getaway car.

Towards twilight time, he parked his car in a lot and strolled onto Grant Avenue. Glowing apricot lanterns festooned arching telephone lines. Discarded red and gold "good luck" money packets were strewn about the street like confetti. The fragrance of fresh flowers was everywhere. The flowers stands were busy—purple plum blossoms (luck), multicolored Chrysanthemums (a good year), and golden sunflowers (health), adorned each.

The apothecary store with its ancient animal cures was better than any shop on Union Square. Vials of ground seal, bear claws, and exotic fish oils always fascinated him. More importantly, there was a meat, fish and poultry store next door that in his mind doubled as a diminutive aquarium cum zoo. The Chinese liked their fish and birds live, looking right at them. They practiced "fresh and local" long before Alice Waters landed in Berkeley.

People were scurrying about attempting to locate a place to observe the oldest Chinese New Year Parade (1853) in the United States. Flags, banners, paper dragons and lions, and crooked politicians in convertible Cadillacs would be winding their way through the throng shortly.

The pride and joy of the parade will always be the St. Mary's Chinese Girls' Drum and Bugle Corps. Back in January of 1961 they stole the show at President Kennedy's inaugural parade. JFK smiled large and clapped loudly as the girls from San Francisco serenaded "When Irish Eyes Are Smiling" in perfect pitch. McNamara and his band wouldn't have had a chance. Even today, it is the only marching band he and his family have ever held in their hearts.

Actually two parades were going to occur this evening. One in his head was going to march to the tune of his absolute favorite five course Chinese banquet, and the other being the actual parade itself, which he'd watch from a second story restaurant window.

When he entered the restaurant and looked it over, he always believed it was impossible to cram any more Far East items on its walls, and to his amazement, there were always more each time he took a meal there. Foot per square foot, no restaurant in the city beat this one for esoteric items. The walls and floors were like a war movie with explosions of color, and he could perceive himself as a sort of courier behind battle lines negotiating tables, plants, and other obstacles until he safely reached his table. He sat down at a small circular table with a lazy Susan condiment center piece. A teapot appeared. A bottle of ginger ale and a fifth of brandy followed, and the feast was on.

A crisp watercress and chestnut salad arrived first. Little Lobos Creek just west of Chinatown in the Presidio played a large part back in the day. Long ago, a classmate's father made a living plucking the watercress from the creek and selling it at the old produce market in front of the Ferry Building.

Shark fin soup followed, and its fragrance rose like music. During his Municipal Pier fishing days, entrepreneurial Samoans canvassed the pier for sharks and bat rays. The Samoans diced the bat ray fins and sold them as "scallops" to anyone interested. The shark fins were sold for soup ingredients.

An order of shrimp was next, and it brought to mind the Shrimp Boat Restaurant on Evans Avenue beside the naval ship yard. While dining at the Shrimp Boat one could watch the Chinese shrimpers separating the ghost shrimp from their nets and walking with basket loads up to the restaurant. There was much bycatch in the nets—crabs and smelt mostly. Their remains were tossed into the drink, attracting game fish, and in turn attracting our gang. On warm summer nights the stripers went wild beside the shrimp piers, like noodles boiling in a pot.

A steaming plate of black mussels was placed before him. The tang of salt water touched his tongue and he reminisced. Low tide days brought out the Pacific Islanders. They'd flip rocks and kelp for cockles and mussels and an occasional bullhead.

A red snapper followed, its head and tail still attached. It signified a beginning and end to the meal. The clear-eyed fish swam in a glistening pool of plum sauce and sea cucumbers. Years ago when the local party boats fished for "rock fish" the only limit was how many the fisherman could carry off of the boat on his back. Burlap sacks of snappers ruled. The effect of this is a wound that will never heal, he thought. A modest 10 fish limit applies these days, along with significant coastal closures as insurance.

All American holidays involve gunpowder. The Chinese New Year Celebration is no exception. Chinatown goes crazy for firecrackers, bottle rockets, anything incendiary. We're not talking about the $29.99 safe and sane "patriot pack" that service clubs shove at us every 4th of July either. We're talking about honest to goodness big bang stuff.

To anyone uninformed, the outbreak of WWIII was at hand. To the informed, the parade was approaching quickly. He felt the percussion aftermaths and the sweet sounds of drums, bugles, and xylophones chiming in. It seems silly to think so, but deep inside he felt an emotional upwelling that made him shiver, quiver with an innate sense of all is well here on earth while the band played on to the illusionary effects of fog-tinted fireworks as a backdrop. It's an only in San Francisco sensation.

The evening of eventualities concluded, another Far East Auld Lang Syne entered the ages. Two fortune cookies were presented to him beside his bill. Some say fortune cookies originated in San Francisco. Some say Los Angles. As far as he could recollect, the cookies were around long before a box of self-serving macaroni positioned itself as "The San Francisco Treat." Later for that noise he thought. He placed one cookie in his shirt pocket, opened the other, ate it, and read its prophesy:

"You regret everything and live in past."

Win some, lose some, he thought and walked out onto to Grant Avenue and headed back to his car. Refreshed, with new found hope he got back inside his vehicle and placed his key in the ignition. It didn't kick over. "What's new," he thought. He got outside and lifted the hood up, even though he had no mechanical savvy whatsoever. It's just what guys did.

Someone had snatched his car battery.

He leaned against the car fender. He crossed his arms and stared at the starless fog-filled sky. He felt the other fortune cookie in his pocket and for no reason at all opened it up, stuffed it in his mouth, and read the following:

"Today is not a good day, tomorrow is not so good either."

# *Fit to be Tied*

The two thugs at his front door started to stomp him almost immediately after he opened it. This kind of thing was not news to him. A week earlier these same two had busted into his apartment. They had planned to burglarize his place and sell his property. To their surprise, the apartment was nearly barren. His furniture had been repossessed. The thugs thought they could bail out the day by drinking his booze. When they opened the fridge door there was only one Kraft cheese single. No sooner had the two thugs left his apartment than they began to plot their revenge for their wasted time. This came in the form of attempting to knock him into next week.

While he was being stomped he remained quiet, like he was the first cousin to a mummy. He was reminiscing, like a year in review thing. He had lost his job during the winter and his wife left him that spring. It enhanced his lifelong belief that he was not fit for anything or anyone.

When he regained consciousness from the drubbing, he felt that his bones and whatever was left of him could be carted off in a burlap sack, and not a big one.

As he administered homemade splints to his arms and legs he thought about a crooked TV preacher he had seen on television waving a Bible and espousing a basic four word philosophy for life: "Things happen, people change." Not for him. He could not believe how long his bad luck had been lasting—since the Eisenhower administration.

He could trace the root cause of his troubles to one simple fact. He

41

was always "out in left field" or "left out" or "leaned to the left." Simply put, he was born left handed and found himself feebly navigating in a right hander's world.

On up through his fifth year in life he appeared to be coasting. Kindergarten changed that. He was artfully putting a Picasso-like stick man together when he experienced his first dose of Catholic corporal punishment and the "three-strike" rule. A penguined nun snuck up from behind him, rapped his knuckles with a ruler, and unkindly advised him he was using "the wrong hand." This was the same nun who asked the class two questions while they stood at attention beside their small stools. The first question was "Who made you?" The class replied "God made us." The second was, "Where is God?" "God is everywhere," they responded. He was always visibly shaken by this. God was apparently watching him use the wrong hand and ratting him out to a mean-spirited enforcer who had a face like the Sphinx. The nun also believed in progressive discipline. The light wrap turned in to an ear twister, and then into a solid tug to the hair. He was slowly being dismembered before the first grade.

When his father took him fishing for the first time he felt he had found his future. That first trip down to the Bay turned complicated when his dad showed him how to tie a fishing knot "the RIGHT way." Pops used his left hand as a vice while the right hand wove an un-intricate square knot. There is this funny thing about his life. He never forgot his first time at anything that developed into a love. He mastered the bird's nest on a knot. This is no small feat. Like the nun who had punched herself silly roughing him up, his father also gave up and let him be.

When he joined the Boy Scouts of America at age 11, he had visions of hiking and camping, but mostly of fishing in the great outdoors. He had no idea that with the great outdoors came a commitment to the great indoors—a weekly meeting. He received a scouting manual at the first meeting. Following the "a Scout is trustworthy" stuff was

Chapter 1: Knot tying. Armed with knot drawings, he took a leap of faith and promptly failed. It was the same left hand hold, right hand weave deal. "Who needs knots in San Francisco?" he thought. He would never receive a merit badge in knot tying nor advance above the entry level rank of "Tenderfoot."

At age 12, he left the wide wonderful world of knots for greener pastures. The green was derived from christenings, weddings and baptisms. He became an altered boy. There were fringe benefits also. The church wine came in one gallon bottles and there was enough back in the vestibule to keep the whole parish corked. It was Tokay, and good. He also learned that gambling (Men's Club Monte Carlo nights and Bingo!), intoxication, and womanizing were all ok and wiped off the slate when you confessed your sins to the priest for a few short Hail Marys.

It was not all coffee and cake though. He was having problems in others areas. In school, the three ring binder was a major menace for a left hander. Cut and paste projects were pitiful, and ended up looking like chop suey. Something as simple as a pair of scissors is a right handed instrument. Another time his father took him bird hunting. Shotguns are designed to eject shells to the right when the gun is placed on the right shoulder. When placed on the left shoulder, a hot burning shell case tattoos the left hander in the mug and a very visible biscuit-sized swelling develops. Once was enough of that noise. Add any visual instruction books also. This would include, but was not limited to: musical instruments, anything mechanical, woodworking, and worst of all for him, fly tying.

He continued to fish though, mostly San Francisco Bay stuff, and almost always amazed himself with his ingenious ability to secure a sinker or a hook to the business end of his line. Each time, the knot was as new to him as the one before it, and would be as unrecognizable as the one that would follow.

In the early '60s, his high school years, a few of the old hounds he hung out with began getting hopped up on hallucinogens. That wasn't his cup of chowder. For a lefty, the world was complicated enough. Why complicate the complicated?

In that same decade, and for reasons not clear to anyone, even today, Uncle Sam decided to give them folks in southeast Asia a good dose of democracy. He decided the safest way to fight "commies" was on a ship. As far he could tell, the Viet Cong had no navy.

One day while at Navy boot camp his platoon marched merrily along into a class entitled Marlinspike Seamanship. From the sound of it, he thought it probably had something to do with marlin fishing at sea. No problems there, he was into that sort of stuff. To his misfortune, the marlinspike turned out to be a thin tool that fashions splices, bends, lashing, and knots to manila, cotton or hemp rope. It was a knot tying class, and it was taught by right handed experts. The instructors had the innate ability whip, weave and whirl a knot unlike any other he had ever seen, and could just as quickly disassemble it with one light line pull.

The day he left they gave him a typewriter.

It's safe to say that in the decades that followed he never picked up A.J. McClane's *Fishing Encyclopedia*, or Lefty Kreh's contributions on famous fishing knots (bowlines, half hitches, bimini twists). Reading "The Knots You Need to Know" would be a Rubik's Cube. He was never destined to be "a knot guy." Not ever.

These days, in the twilight of life's knots, he could stand tall. He had perfected just one knot. It meant something to him, he had finally mastered one. It would make lefties proud. This knot was easily recognizable to him and all others. Best of all, it could come in all sorts of forms and figures. More importantly it untied itself in one quick deft motion. He christened it the "knife knot" because that's all it took to undo it.

# *Hopeless*

When his uneducated grandfather got off the boat from Venice, Italy, he went to work for *"La Famiglia,"* the mob, in Mountain View. Nonno—his grandfather—operated a still during Prohibition. In less than one year's time, his grandfather's picture grace-noted the first page of the *San Jose Mercury News*. The still blew up. His grandfather suffered first degree burns, and spent six months in the slammer. The family name was further besmirched when his grandfather moved to San Francisco in 1930. Live poultry was brought into the city daily back then, and his grandfather became a convicted chicken thief.

When folks glanced at his car, one thought came to mind: how many people were hurt in that wreck? His living quarters were equally dismal. Skid row was a step up. His hard work ethic was weak, and his looks never rated a second glance. He had become the first cousin of a human crash test dummy. Hopeless.

He was continually thinking of ways to change his life and lifestyle, perhaps by going north and chaining himself to an old growth redwood, or anchoring himself to rock beneath a proposed dam. Of course saving seals and whales was an option, but none were close at hand. The ocean was a logistical issue. Peace marches always turned out violent. Protest vigils at San Quentin were cold, while nuclear and civil rights demonstrations were disastrous. There were enough lost causes going around, and he was one of them.

His hopelessness could be easily explained. What little extra loot he had in life was spent on fishing tackle. He collected "stuff" like no other angler on earth, and worse, for all the wrong reasons. Someday, somewhere, he just "might need it." Complicating matters, were his angling abilities; he had no idea what he was doing, yet his incompetence never prevented him from plunging into an angling purchase with enthusiasm.

It all started with dreams, and he had plenty of them. He believed that "dreams could come true" with a credit card, or cash on the barrelhead.

In the good-old-days, his exuberance was held at bay by the monthly distribution of sporting magazines, the occasion foray to a sporting goods store, or a close-out sale in the newspapers. His wants were regulated by the times, and of course he still had room to add to his collection. The internet changed that. He bought a computer.

It's been said that the only true way to know the edge is to go over it. He did, in the form of Amazon, eBay, Yahoo!, and any other online purveyor who catered to his angling needs. The packages and parcels that appeared on his doorstep bore postage marks from all seven continents, and just like that, he ran out of room.

Like Edison and the light bulb, he discovered a way to make room for more merchandise. He sold his stuff back online, and almost always at a great loss.

He had the fever. One that Dr. Phil could not diagnose. Dr. Dean Adele hung up on him, and a TV evangelist could offer little help. The online auction house action had a hold on him.

Making matters worse, his landlord upped his rent, assuming that he could afford more by virtue of the unending stream of packages arriving daily. The UPS and FedEx drivers, beneath their breath, took to calling him and his family members mean names. The mailman was pissed off too. His boss, the district manager of the door-to-door salesmen's outfit he worked for consoled him for his lack of productivity. His sales were near nonexistent. He sold parakeet training tips on DVD.

Bernard Malamud once wrote that for a story to become a story, something has to change. It did. His breakthrough became possible when he joined Online Auction Anonymous, a twelve step program, online. Through group meetings and the peer pressure of the like-minded, the packages containing all things angling began to subside.

These days, if he goes online at all, its always near noon, and almost always with his group. His online auction action is at bay, at least for the time being.

# Galloping Nervosa

It was one of those rare once a winter mornings in San Francisco when a frost had formed and crusted into ice, locking the city's sidewalks and trees in a thin film that usually burned off by noon.

When he got up that morning and looked at himself in the mirror, it was clear he had the appearance of a crazy man with a 60s stroke look about him. It had been one of those full moon, "me against the moon" nights when every nightmare imaginable came to visit him. A major bout with booze earlier that evening didn't help things either.

There was a banging inside his temples, something akin to small sledgehammer blows. Someone had stuck cactus in his eyes, he thought. His breathing was heavy, large gulps of air were necessary, and his heart was banging away like a good thumping from Attila the Hun.

Perhaps a copy of *Gray's Anatomy* would have helped explain these symptoms, he thought, but a copy was not at hand. Besides, he felt he was pretty good at self examination and diagnosis. He watched a lot of *General Hospital*. As best as he could recollect, there was an episode on season #7 that made mention of *galloping nervosa*. There was absolutely no question in his mind that his symptoms were comparable. Three more things: he was neurotic, dramatic, and had a penchant to complicate the most uncomplicated matters.

His small world whirled, and he felt the need to sit down. He went to his one comfortable chair that faced the lone window in his apartment. The window faced a brick wall. He removed the remains of a mail order cheese log and two empty cans of malt liquor from the fridge and sat down and looked outside.

With an expressionless face he stared at the wall like it was the Great one in China. With his end imminent, he reasoned it was time to get his affairs in order and to make arrangements.

The notion that there would be no ocean beside a big beautiful bay where he was headed was just as great as the loss of its touch, its feel, and the tang of salt air from all angles.

Unexpectedly, tears started falling, and he began recalling the good things he was gonna miss.

He thought first of summer, when the unsung coastline held great balls of bait fish, and anchovies rested in breakers. Big schools of bass scouring the shoreline pushed the fish up to the surface and towards shore, and seagulls from above became dive bombers. The frenzied bait fish and the bass in hot pursuit would run up into the foam line and beach themselves. Surfcasters complicated the melee, battling each other, and a treacherous undertow, for a limit of three fat fish in rapid succession.

Jack O'Neill's surf shop was a sand dune away from the water's edge. Jack perfected and patented the first neoprene wetsuit for surfers and cold water surfcasters. Jack shuffled south to Santa Cruz in the '60s and never looked back. The motto for his cold water suits was simple, "It's always summer inside."

The rocks at Seal Rock and Camel Back, beneath the Cliff House were good places to stare at ships doing what they do. On occasion an errant salmon swam by, halibut too, and the plug casters clobbered them. You could get good clams and cockles in the rock crevices too.

The tides seemed to be turning in his head. He felt a need to lie down until the clarions called him home.

By the way, a warm winter sun had veined the ice outside and small rivulets began to run.

He started to think about "the other side" things, like how big of a halo would he receive? Would his wings fit properly? What size cloud would he rest on? This music worried him; was a harp easier to play than a trumpet?

He thought about the warm white sand at Baker Beach, prettier in person than any postcard could print. When he was a kid it was unfishable to all but the fleet afoot, those adept at dodging the military police. It was a US Army installation back then. These days it's the principal jewel in the city's national park.

Lands End beneath the golf course was always a challenge, but repelling down for a sack of rockfish was reward enough. In earlier times there was no limit, and that's why there are no fish to speak of today.

China Beach below the sophisticated Sea Cliff charms anyone who has been there. It's a sheltered beach below a steep precipice, with plenty of perch and Dungeness crabs in season.

He was close to a daylight dream, drifting into the fascination and wonder of the golden gateway, aptly named by army Captain John Fremont, 91 years before the big bridge stole its name and thunder.

The black rocks beneath the bridge are home to octopus, eels, and ling cod. At low tide the Chinese "poke polers" slip a piece of squid fastened to a long length of bamboo cane into the seaweed and sludge, and yank out an unlucky cod.

The sun was high in the winter sky when he woke up. His biggest surprise was that he was still alive, and, well, feeling well. Happy hour at the local pub was just about to happen, and all the old hounds he hung out with were already there.

The sidewalks were wet as he splashed towards the tavern. He had a new lease on life. He felt like dancing. He wished he could toe tap like Gene Kelly in *Singin' in the Rain*, or maybe Judy Garland and the rest of the yellow brick road gang. But then again, maybe a little soul searching was in order. He began thinking about a battered and bruised Don Quixote, whose last line to sidekick Sancho Panza was simply "It's been said the greatest victory in life is the victory over yourself."

This evening was going to be different. Tonight it's gonna be bottled water, carrot juice, anything but alcohol.

# The Reel Deal

The holiday season was coming up quickly. He could tell by the amount of empty libations left beside the roadways. Times were good, he thought, and his aluminum can collecting business was going great. Great success was coming quickly he thought. Soon, he would be a man of leisure and have the means to pursue a sporting life.

He felt a compelling urge to splurge. He had always been interested in fishing, fly fishing in particular. He was going to buy a fly rod and reel. Years ago when he saw *A River Runs Through It* with Brad Pitt, it was easy for him to insert himself on the silver screen beside Brad.

"Whoa Brad I gotta another 18" whooper!"

"Super duper pard, lets call it quits, slip into Tinseltown and hit on some starlets."

"Deal me in. Fishing's my middle name, but starlets are my game."

Back in the old days, when he was a wino down on skid row, any thoughts that came into his mind were usually put into action. Immediately. Usually, with disastrous results. These days, his logic was reasoned, seasoned by time. He was a businessman, and would do nothing to besmirch the good name of his business, "Worldwide Recycling." Why give those old hounds back at the soup kitchen something to talk about? And besides, in the back of his mind he could see himself on Oprah, as the star of some feel good segment. He was a big picture guy. He could see himself writing a screenplay about his life. He thought two time Academy Award winner Robert

De Niro could fill his shoes perfectly.

"So Bob, what did you think of the script?"

"You aced it ace, let's start the cameras rolling"

"Calm down Bobby, first things first. I'll have my lawyers draw up the contract docs ASAP."

The Friday night gang usually whoops it up pretty good on the streets of San Francisco, making Saturday morning the most solid day to collect. It wasn't easy for him, nor for his entrepreneurial spirit, to head downtown on a bus and bypass all those stout malt liquor cans lying resting in the gutters, but he was going downtown to buy a fly rod and reel.

His mind began to drift, and, just like that, a very light Rip Van Winkle snooze snuck up on him. Doze, no doze, that sort of thing. When the bus passed the Russian Embassy he thought back to the good days when the Ruskies were good, and honest enemies. Sneaking around talking into shoe phones, infiltrating and collecting everyday espionage for who knows what, and why? These days, Uncle Sam is selling Kentucky Fried Chicken alongside the Kremlin. They are our comrades now. He missed those cold war commies.

The bus wheezed up towards the top of Nob Hill. Back in high school his classmates and he took their prom dates to dinner at the Fairmont Hotel's Tonga Room. The Tonga is a Tiki lounge located in the hotel basement. It's the old Fairmont swimming pool. The walls are adorned with grass shacks, sacred volcanoes and hula girls, and back then, a banner overhead identified the bar as the "Gateway to the Pacific." A live band was tugged to and fro across the pool on a genuine synthetic Hawaiian war canoe. The band played Don Ho music on request, and a garden hose on high lightly spritzed the crowd to create a rain forest effect. The thing he remembered most about his prom experience was all the girls retiring to the powder room to freshen up. His date didn't return. He spent the evening there with a $4.00 corsage and two Shirley Temples.

Later on in life, during a particularly dreary winter evening he needed warmth. He felt the South Seas throbbing in his veins. He needed a minor miracle to pull this one off, one like the three loaves of bread and fish that fed the throng in Nazareth. His $9 wouldn't get him to the end of the rapid transit line. He soothed himself by sliding down one Singapore Sling at the Tonga Room's "Hurricane Bar" beside the water hose rain forest.

He got off the bus at 3rd and Market, bound for glory at a trout fly shop in downtown San Francisco, 60 miles from the nearest mayfly hatch.

He had been so far from flush for so long that he decided he'd shoot the moon. Absolutely no expense would be spared for a first class USA made rod and reel. The Popeil pocket fisherman, or a blister pack Snoopy rod and reel combo were stone age stuff. He planned to light the cash register up to the tune of $39.00, including tax.

Entering the fly shop he approached the glass case containing the fly reels. That's where the good stuff is, like in a jewelry store, or an exhibition of Tut's Tomb's finest. One thing was for sure, his reel had to have a ratchet. All high quality fly reels have ratchets. He was nobody's fool.

If it is possible to be locked into a place, a time, and a moment, he was. He became a human mannequin. Reel sticker shock does that to the uninformed. His blood pressure elevated, his throat went dry, his body wouldn't budge. A police stun gun would give you the same effect.

His eyes had the surprised wide-eyed look of a bug that met a windshield at 60 miles per hour. If you were wondering how long he stood staring at the glass case, the Big Bang Theory would be a good place to start.

After the dinosaurs had vanished and Rome ruled the world he could feel movement in his eyes. Glancing slowly from side to side he exercised his sockets and refocused on the reel case. There was a gold anodized salt water model with 3 adjustable speeds. It was called the "Hercules" and beside it sat its freshwater brother, the "Samson." It had a ratchet. Both were marked as close outs at $599 and $499, respectively. A clerk asked him if he needed help. He sure did, because he couldn't speak, but he shook his head no.

Around the Renaissance he began to sweat profusely. He had become entranced by the astounding nomenclature and reel names. Magnesium frames, clutch ball bearings, conical, ceramic coated 747 stopping drag systems with a show stopping model moniker like the "Magnitude," the "Momentum," the "Mach I" or the "Lightspeed." These reels are designed to make mincemeat out of Melville's Moby.

Columbus had discovered the new world by the time store employees had him sitting down with a cold compress on his noggin, and Neil Armstrong had walked on the moon by the time he returned to his semi-normal state.

Walking back to the bus he wondered how he could explain this to anyone, anywhere. Perhaps, only Peter Pan would understand.

# Love Affairs

Storm clouds rolled in and up over the California coastline as he pulled into his driveway that Friday night. He got out of his car, and walked towards his "home," which these days was nothing more than a house. In his mind he was going over the list of things he needed to forget about her, things like the push and shove of their love affair.

He walked up to the front door, opened it and looked inside at the phone. You'd have thought by now he would be used to being home alone, with not one message on the phone. He turned on the radio, the lights low, and poured himself a small glass of wine, "refrigerator red," he called it. Once the bottle was opened, it went to rot quickly, unless refrigerated. Immediately.

Tonight was gonna be different, no more tears. Time to think of other things, he thought. His second UFO sighting for instance. Life never got weird enough for him. It wasn't anything he could talk to anyone about because, well, there was no one to talk to.

The truth is, he needed to get a hold of himself, or someone else. He called an acquaintance (friends were in short supply), and got the recorder. He called another, and the same thing occurred. No one is home these days he thought, except him, and he did not care to converse with machinery.

A second glass of wine started to work its way into his system. He should get some rest, the following day he would be fishing. Aside from her, it was the other twin tributary of his life and times on earth. He could always count on fishing to pull him through. Fishing was enduring, durable, solid—like breakfast, something he could always depend on.

Lying in bed, his beating heart brought him back to her. The two of them both knew that each of them could not allow the other to be themselves in some situations. Because of this, an act, a look, or a comment was enough to start something, or have it lay latent, to be used later in an arsenal of adjectives designed to destroy the other.

"Enough of this noise" he said to no one. He had to get up early, rise with the spring bud break, and hopefully, a trout or two would rise also. There was always this thing about fishing, it was never really a "getaway" for him, more like a "get into" thing. Also, if you were like him, it might make you less aware that your heart is a very sad affair.

The fishing that day was not as good as it gets. The water was high and brown from runoff. But he had no recall at all of last night. This is the effect that fishing had on him. Driving home was another matter. He drove a long way going the wrong way. Old loves don't let loose easily.

Once he reached home he sensed that the evening would repeat itself, like Bill Murray in the movie *Groundhog Day*. Not tonight though, this would be a night to shelter his heart in some safe harbor.

While reaching into the refrigerator to retrieve the jug the phone rang. It was you know who.

Clear springtime rivers were going to run again.

# The Romance of Opening Day

*It's been said that in the spring a young man's fancy turns to love,
and, if there is any time left over, he just may try a little trout fishing.*

Here on earth, no one has an exemption from sorrow. Last year a friend had been going through a steady succession of the Ds nothing serious like death, or disease; minor Ds though, things like, depression, a minor health disorder, and the worst one, divorce, a wound that never seems to heal in some. They say that "forever" in a California marriage is about five years. His forever lasted three months. His wife had left him a note and simply vanished with the pizza guy.

Looking back on his life he was never ever one of those laughter, happy-ever-after types. He had issues. One symptom can only be described as "the droop," and that needs no explanation. As for looks, someone started stealing his hair when he was in his teens, and his teeth had these amazing configurations that seemed to change every time he smiled, which wasn't very often. He described himself as heavy set, and that was true. He had a whole lot of love to give because there was a whole lot of him.

Traditionally, we two did a he and me rendezvous on the eve of opening day in late-April, somewhere, anywhere where water flowed and fish were willing. This year would be no different. Hopefully there was no high water up in Dunsmuir, "Where the Sacramento River is a Trout Stream." It was only natural for me to assume that he needed my support and guidance to help him through his hard times. I'm a good listener, and nine times out of ten, I give good advice. Although one time, I got a call from another friend who was considering ending it all. After listening to his dilemma, I told him it was certainly an option. With regrets, I should mention that he took it. For some time after that all my advice stayed on the safe side: the weather, favorite show tunes, sports, those kinds of things.

We agreed to meet in Dunsmuir at the Dear John Letter Lounge on Main Street the night before the opener. A motel room within walking distance of the bar was easily arranged. I was not expecting any good news from him. I had brought a half pint of V.O. to cushion any curves in our conversations. I knocked back a strong snort before I left the motel room. The whiskey started kicking in as I sauntered down to the saloon. It worked wonders for me. I could hear pool balls busting, and a juke box blasting some country and western lament. The lyrics had a thing or two to do with lost love, found again, lost again, and a dog named "Shep."  If you understand country and western music, which I do, "hurtin" laments are number one with these folks.

There was a banner above the bar entrance that read:

## LIVE MUSIC TONIGHT!
### POOT "THE TRUTH" PEARSON
### & HIS PLACERVILLE PLAYBOYS
## COME INSIDE AND HEAR THE TRUTH!

The gang inside was an uncomplicated lot. Tom Foolery, and Friday night fun reigned. I of course was looking for a basket case. My friend, affectionately known as "Porky."

I sat on a bar stool and ordered a water high, and waited for him to show up. I watched the dance floor. There was a smooth dancing couple, dancing buckle to buckle to a nice toe tapper. My foot got happy too. I can tap my foot with the best of them. The song concluded and the bartender/MC popped on the stage to announce "radio and recording stars," Poot and the Playboys. The dance floor started filling up and Poot and the boys launched into a barn burner. "Well it won't be but a week or two, you'll be out loving someone new," the opening stanza seemed to enliven all hands. The joint started jumping, as they listened to "The Truth."

A circle of hand clappers formed on the floor, they were egging something on. Curiosity killed the cat, information brought him back. I snuck a peek in between two people. There was a guy (dancing?) to his own tune. An organ grinder's monkey would be no match for this bird. He was shaking it like Elvis shook it. A corn, a bunion, or a blister forming on his feet stood no chance. His feet did not touch the ground. As the song was ending the crowd started applauding and this guy yelled out "Wait till you see the next dance, you've never see anything like it!"  And I am certain they hadn't. His voice had a familiar ring. It was the Porker. He asked Poot for a drum roll, raised his hands up to halt it, and introduced the crowd to a big-haired red head that was every bit his equal size-wise. She was his "fiancée" and he had met her at the Dear John the day before. Who knew?  He said she knew every song on the juke box by heart and that they were "partner-in-life's." He also said she was a Dunsmuir "virgin"—she had three adult children, and two grandchildren.

He asked Poot to pick up the tempo. Poot put out a yodel and went into a rousing rendition of "Bring it on down to my house baby, ain't nobody home but me."  The Flying Wallendas would have watched in wonder, and John Travolta would be jealous. Those two had dance fever.

Besides his bride-to-be, Pork had made major adjustments that reflected a positive self image. For instance, there was some kind of animal pelt perched on his cabeza, and a snazzy set of new teeth to match his smile. There was also a red rag top in the parking lot.

Later that evening we three talked about the old times and created a new one. We agreed to meet on the river behind the city ballpark where Babe Ruth and his boys played a game back in the '20s when they barnstormed the country. By the way, the Bambino belted one out that day.

Pork never showed the next day. This is what loves does to you.

I haven't seen or heard from him since. Someone said the two had headed off to Hollywood. They intended to dance on TV.

This a variant factor of the Ds I had mentioned earlier. It appears that it infected the two of them. We call it the "Dreamer's Disease."

# His Own Private Sky

He sat on a high bluff above the creek, drinking in a fading night's overture. Screeching night noises in the woodlands below began to subside. Daylight was well on its way, and with it, his own private sky. Another streamside sonata was set to start. Songbirds and raptors would serenade the hillsides looking for love, and he would launch himself deep into the canyon crease.

A short snort of Seagram's was essential to get his head clear and he took a pull. You could say it was an old family tradition, because it was. It had been the kind of week in the city that knocked him into the following week—neutron bomb-like noise, mind numbing clatter, chatter, and a vortex of combustible engines, high speed siren chases, and human beings habitually racing over one another for that last piece of cheese. He would end the week's worth of urban arrogance with the hope and chance of catching a trout or two. An overnighter, the sort of "Hello I must be going" sortie that city dwellers are so accustomed to.

A light breeze blew its way up the canyon. It was good news. The wind at his back would assist his ascent up the creek trail. Cotton clouds and blue skies crowned the high country peaks. If the creek didn't rise, and the trout did, all things on earth would be aces.

There was always a touch of Hemingway's big two-fisted *Big Two-Hearted River* running through the tributaries of his head to his heart. The aloneness of it. The solitary angler not escaping from human nature, but escaping into mother's nature.

He moved slowly up the mountain. Midway, he took a short pause for the cause, relieved himself, and sat down. While looking over the landscape a daydream began. It was New Age jive that was incomprehensible to him on any level. For instance, his aura or inner chi and things like his life flow. He was of another era, one prefaced with old, old five and dimers, old folks, old school, and a black and white world when he needed it. On the other hand, there were times that he needed Technicolor, wide screen stuff, and a short snort seemed to see him through those times. He reached into his backpack and took another blast.

Back on the trail, and ever upward, his mind meandered again. Not long ago, at a fish show, he had been swept away by a smooth speaking salesman who's pitch was the big briny, some high octane salt water sideshow battling meat eating beasts that meant business. It's not a low rent look at life to pull out a piece of plastic to fly off to St. Somewhere and do battle, but the notion of a real live ocean was appealing.

Two things took place on that trip. The first thing that occurred was the financial burden that the trip placed on his credit card. These days paradise must be paid off, with interest. The second thing that took place was 16 hours of high and pressurized travel over 5 time changes for a spot of sport fishing that didn't pan out, and remarkably, this had no effect on him. As odd as it seems the motion of a rolling ocean was no bother either. There was, though, something intrinsic inside him that made him physically ill.

It was a heartache that hurt so bad that it can only be described as a medical condition, a broken heart, that stemmed from the grief and betrayal of his beloved trout. To him, this emotional two timing a rainbow trout for others out there on the high seas was a breach of faith to his first love. In his mind, this neurosis led him to emotional and mental disorders that could only be cured with a healthy helping of the high country back home.

And so it was that he reached his spot near noon, rolled out his sleeping bag, and with another affectionate nod to Nick Adams, removed a big can beans from his backpack. He consumed the contents cold, slowly, as if he were eating caviar. Fortified, he rigged up his fly rod. He fashioned a fly to the leader. It was of his own creation. He called it "the kitchen sink" for no other reason than that he had used everything at hand to fabricate the fly. Then he went fishing.

The fish were fickle that day. There was no jubilation, nothing to rejoice over, just a nice day of light contemplation while casting over smooth currents. The sun started to slip over the windward side of the mountain, and shadows lengthened over the landscape. A slight reflexive shiver overcame him.

A stiff drink was easily arranged, and another followed. He glowed, peacefully, beside the alpenglow of a glorious afternoon.

He really hit the drink towards twilight, a head first, face down, flop baptizing by non-healing waters. From the tip of his toes, to his nose, he froze, appearing something akin to the first cousin of a block of ice. He skedaddled to the camp site and bed, safe, warm and dry once more.

That night he placed his hands behind his head and watched a light show that had nothing to do with headlights, spotlights, or candlelight. It was starlight. A super nova slid across the skyline while a small shooting star burned bright, like a roman candle, extinguishing itself after a brief beginning. He was going to save this one, savor it, some kind of souvenir he thought, and he surrendered to a sweet sleep.

A light breeze whistling in the pine trees suggested strings, mandolins, woodwinds, playing memorable and moving moments, in concert with the great outdoors.

Dawn broke bleakly. Grey cloud cover had masked the mountain top and there was something in the wind that suggested an ill-meaning morning. He broke camp to a dropping barometric pressure, and headed down the hill.

Walking rapidly he watched the clouds above collapse, disintegrate and reemerge, driven by some sort of tempestuous force. Incremental raindrops fell as he topped the trailhead. He stopped and looked back. The light mandolin winds of last night had become an increasing crescendo of bugle thunder that bellowed across the canyon and into the plains below. The symphonic sounds were a perfect pitch accompaniment and the finale to his own private sky.

# Victory in Defeat

In late fall he walked west, into the wind and up along the creek. When he reached a small clearing he stopped and walked in a small circle, north, east, south and west. He had read once that this ritual would give his day "balance." This was Red Man lore, and apparently something the Indians practiced daily, up until the white man started shooting them in the ass, ripping-off their land, and forcing them to run for cover.

Early morning west winds always blew down the canyon, while the afternoon wind blew up the canyon. It was some sort of thermal effect that occurred when the valley heated up during daylight. This phenomena was just fine with him. It allowed him to walk into the wind and get close to small unsuspecting furbearing animals. He had a specialty in that field also, the Weasel family. He was on familiar footing when it came to these critters in forests, and he had met many, face to face, in every urban environment he had ever been in.

As was his custom, he did not expect to encounter fabulous fishing. The night before, the moon had been as bright as a reading light. Translation: The "No fish full moon swoon" period. No problems here though, he had an outside chance. At home the night before he took the only medicine he needed, a healthy dose of Dr. Needham's *Trout Streams* treatise. It was the cure for the who, what, where, when, and why of all things trout.

He was en route to one particular pool, that held one particular trout. A rainbow, that was no *Field & Stream* contest winner, nor wall mount, but a semi-respectable-sized fish of 17 or 18 inches. In his lifetime he had caught larger, longer, and heavier fish. But this one, living in a narrow channel beneath a small waterfall, had been a six month pursuit, somewhat akin to Ahab and his fish, but as you can imagine, on a much smaller scale. More importantly, he had gotten back in touch with Dr. Needham's master work, *Trout Streams*, and its who, what, when, where, and why, committing most of it to memory.

His first encounter with this fish took place in early spring when the *Skwala* stoneflies were climbing out of the streambed to do what most do in the spring. The fish would dash out from beneath the falls, snatch a nymph off the waters and retreat to its lair. No problem here he thought, a *Skwala* nymph dead drifted would match this hatch. One fishless hour, and two hundred casts later, the trout had not shown itself. This rainbow thought he was a selective brown trout. Really.

In May and June he waited and watched while the fish picked off pale morning duns, with an occasional golden stone nymph. He countered with PMD emergers, pheasant tail nymphs, and gold stimulators. And he received the same results. Zilch.

In July the green caddis and olive caddis came out, and he heaved elk hair caddis and Bird's Nests at this beauty while the fish sauntered around the slipstream, pell-mell, soliciting the real McCoy, oblivious to any intrusions.

He nearly cracked in August after a bout with size 22 ascending midges failed to generate any enthusiasm. At home that night, voices advised him that he needed a Needham refresher. Diligent research revealed the October caddis would show itself in late fall, and this would be his last chance at this fish committing unintentional harakiri.

And so it went that the fish hit an orange stimulator on his first toss, and the thin thread, not much stronger than a spider web, separated. He watched the fish vault, somersault and vanish. The fight ended in its beginning.

When walking back downstream he started to do what he does best, daydream. He started thinking about Rocky Balboa and how old Rock had his clock cleaned by Apollo Creed in *Rocky I*. Rocky was bruised, battered, and had the look of a human punching bag. He'd survived twelve punishing rounds, and still stood tall.

Yep, he knew just how the Italian Stallion felt. He had just experienced victory in defeat.

# La Luna

## Monsters and Full Moon Fishing

Even now, over 50 years later, he still winces at the thought of it all. Boy Scout Troop #154 held their weekly meetings on Friday nights in the parish hall. He was 10 years old. Up until that time, he had held the night sky in an overarching awe. His Italian grandparents planted, fished and hunted by *"plenilunio,"* the full moon.

Lon Chaney, Boris Karloff, and Bela Lagousi changed all that. Channel 2 in Oakland came into being with one late Friday night program called "Creature Features," and it changed life as he knew it. On an old black and white screen this crew—the Werewolf, Frankenstein, or Count Dracula—committed mayhem on an unsuspecting public, more often than not, beneath a mist-shrouded moon. The full moon made these monsters go crazy.

After a few Friday night episodes watching this gang destroy whole villages, his leisurely stroll home after the Boy Scout meeting became a haul-ass, head-down run to safety. Any thoughts of future trick-or-treating were out of the question. When the moon was out in full force, he was in. Inside. Safe inside his home with saints and guardian angels overhead, crucifixes, a true "good ghost" in the form of his family's religious belief in "the holy ghost," and garlic bulbs. Just the right stuff to ward off any surprises.

Another thing, he had no control over his dreams. He was just in them. He preferred dreams about Knights of the Round Table, good magical wizards like Merlin, castles, and that sort of thing. Usually though, one of the creature feature gang would always inject himself into the picture and terrorize that chivalrous set. As if things were not complicated enough, more often than not, he began to wonder if his grandparents were affiliated with those full moon thugs. Didn't they become full moon activated? Was grandma Dracula's prom date in another life? Who knows? And in whom could he confide?

On the full moon his grandfather riddled the oak wine barrels in their basement. He also planted row crops, biennials, and perennials by the light of the moon. One time his grandfather went off for a bit of nocturnal angling. He remembers it well. The moon that night was the shrimp-like color of playdough. When his grandfather returned home, the back of his pickup truck was filled with striped bass. The fish were the size of first graders. His grandfather was apparently an early practitioner of catch and release. In those days they called it "letting the little ones go."

Just like that, he developed faith in the strange. It was the summer he became welded to moonlight and water. His house was two blocks from the Bay, and any moon hung for howling suited him just fine. He went fishing. He fished on a landfill across a small inlet from the Hunters Point Naval Shipyard. Back then the shipyard was at full force with 10,000 workers working round the clock. Large cranes and lights on dry docked ships shimmered while the moonlight worked its allurement and magic on the still bay waters. It was a far contrast from the afternoon bay zephyrs that produced wind stolen casts. The truth is, he never caught one fish worth talking about. A redtail perch, a smelt or two, and shiners totaled the summer's catch. Skill had always been a stranger to him, and if folks asked "How did you do last night?" his standard response was firm, negligent and untruthful. "I got a limit" he would reply. He would have qualified as a delegate to a national fish liar's club if there was such a thing.

As time moved on and he got older, he bought a skiff and fished the Bay nearly every day. His mother thought he had gills. He learned that you caught the most fish on a following sea, that the last two hours of the incoming tide were the most productive and that the four and five foot tides of summer were sissies compared to the wintertime seven and eight footers. There was a correlation to the moons pull during the winter that produced these humdingers, and if it was legal, he was out there, somewhere, doing what came naturally to him.

He paid little attention to the truth or logic of John Alden Knight's Solunar Tables, a popular fishing book based on the moon. The "me against the moon" theory was for other folks. It was too complicated for him. He had his own simplistic compass.

On still waters, he noted during daylight, that no moon, or a sliver of a moon were best for fishing and that to fish or hunt during a first quarter, a full, or last quarter moon was particularly hopeless. The full moon surprises people, fish, and animals he thought. It also drove them nuts if they spend to much time beneath it.

After over fifty years of fishing he walks around on land where the lunatic is normal. He still goes fishing on a full moon at night. It's called lunacy.

# An Angling Journal

Long ago, and not so very far away (1970 and at the west end of the casting pools) I was brushing up on my casting strokes on a midsummer evening. Hemingway said, "always mention the weather." So I'll do that now. San Francisco has two climates: cool and cold. It was cold; a drizzling gray fog surrounded me and the air was perfumed with the essence of eucalyptus.

On the pathway behind Horner's Corner I heard the approaching sounds of shouting, roaring and howling. It was a male voice, an artillery crash of words that quoted everything and everybody: poetry, sarcasm, statistics, history, blasphemy and wound up with a grand war whoop for free speech, free schools, the glorious bird of America and the principles of Eternal Justice.

I recognized a ranter.

The voice appeared in the form of a short squat cherubic man with a face that glowed like a red bourbon lantern. He had that early-40s heart attack look. He wore a stylish bush jacket, matching tan ascot, upcountry trousers and shoes with enough dirt on them to be reclassified as taxable real estate.

Armed with a fly rod, he began to cast, inaccurately and inelegantly. To no one in particular he shouted: "night squadron forward and step lightly over the wounded men!" I feared for my life. Here was a man who could talk me to death. As I attempted to briskly walk past him, he spun around and pronounced, "Pultroon's the name, angling my game." His voice had the ring of 100 proof. His easy working jaw identified himself as Paul N. Pultroon, a member of the "healing community" by profession. He said it was poor policy to have a snort in front of a fellow angler and offered me a tug. I respectfully declined as he produced a half pint and took what he described as a modest pull. Not coming up for air, he launched into a travelogue of the places, faces, and "somewheres" he had fished. I, of course, was looking up at the sky pretending it was the Sistine Chapel. For the next three decades, I scattered like shrapnel when this monster in a human suit was on the premises or at large nearby.

The major mysteries in my life are as follows: How did he get my phone number? Why me? And why do I receive an early a.m. phone call near Opening Day of the now year round trout season? Each year I'm surprised that he is still alive. We last spoke in the spring of '99. He recited the same old litanies. I practiced good citizenship and listened. Paul said he was calling it a career and giving up angling. At the urging of anonymous family members he was honoring a commitment to his ministry at a small private insane asylum in southern California. On behalf of our fellowship over the years he was forwarding to me his angling journal.

The journal arrived in the form of a black and white flecked book marked "English Composition" on the front cover. In memoriam/celebration I poured an honest slug of vino, sat down and began to page through. The frontispiece reflected a nocturnal camping scene. Beneath an inscription read:

*Dedicated to all my angling brothers and sisters who, like I, have been fortunate enough to sleep beneath the whisk of a comet, a deep throw of stars, a cedar needle mattress and a quickwater trout stream at hand.*
*—Paul N. Pultroon, Esq.*

The journal began on the banks of the Susan River just outside Lassen Park, circa 1966. Paul comments on glacial rock laminates, alpine and sub-alpine belts and briefly mentions a red breasted nuthatch, adding to his life list of bird sightings. It concludes with the following:

| Trout Hooked | Trout Landed |
|:---:|:---:|
| 13 | 0 |

The spring of '69 describes an eventful trip to Tuolumne Meadows above Yosemite with the notation:

| Trout Hooked | Trout Landed |
|:---:|:---:|
| 9 | 0 |

The fall of '73 finds our man on the banks of the Klamath River following a well-hooked steelhead downstream and approaching a hard right turn. His comment, "The steelie was going so fast (and I can provide sworn testimony) that the fish 'missed the turn' and momentarily beached itself on the far bank."

| Steelhead Hooked | Steelhead Landed |
|:---:|:---:|
| 1 | 0 |

The summer of '84 mentions a trout trip on the Truckee. The summation:

| Trout Hooked | Trout Landed |
|:---:|:---:|
| 11 | 0 |

| Birds Hooked | Birds Landed |
|:---:|:---:|
| 1 | 0 |

(Calaveras warbler on a back cast)

I slammed the book shut. It was making me silly in the head. Late-April found me answering a late night, collect phone call from Orange County. Would I accept the charges from a Paul N. Pultroon? I asked the operator if she would be kind enough to ask the caller his middle name, the "N." A minute later she returned with "Nocatchum sir, his middle name is Nocatchum. Indian, I believe." I declined the call, hung up, disconnected the line and changed my number that morning.

# A Mint Condition Winston

Early one Spring morning, the boys at the Angler's Lodge were attacking a box of donuts. They ate like pigs. I ate more (before they had showed up) and went out on the rock wall to digest. Overlooking the ponds, I reflected on my life so far. Two-timing women, three-day bar binges, and second-hand pickup trucks with bad transmissions. As I was sitting there I was approached by a nondescript, totally anonymous looking chap. The best way I could describe him is that you have to look up his picture in your high school yearbook to place the face, despite the fact that you had four years of school together.

He said he had a bamboo fly rod for sale. He'd lost his dot-com job. His rent was overdue and he was desperate to liquidate all his assets. The rod, a family heirloom had been passed down to him from his father and his father's father. I'd heard this one before. Grandpa's antique fly rod usually turns out to be a hacked-up mass produced unidentifiable model, or worse — a 1950s Japanese import.

I thought I'd humor this rube, "whatayahave?" I responded. "A mint condition Winston bamboo fly rod" he replied. Fortunately I had sunglasses on. He went on to say that it was a lightweight trout model and had been built by the San Francisco boys. I was giving him my best disinterested poker face. I lapsed when I reached for a smoke. I gave up smoking thirty years ago.

"I need at least $150 for it. Do you think it's possible?" he asked. I said I didn't think so. And added that it was his good fortune to have contacted me first, as the other boys around here would try to "beat 'em down" on the price. Further that my sense of fair play for my fellow man would not allow me to take advantage of a man in distress.

"$50 is all it's worth" I replied. I launched into a long discussion of how bamboo had fallen out of favor and graphite was now the rage.

"Would you be buying for you?" he asked.

"No way" I shot back. "I'd give it to my grandkids to catch bluegills."

"You seem like a nice guy, you gotta deal; it's in my car."

As we walked to his car my old bones felt like launching into a Gene Kelly "Dancing in the Rain" number. I was the pet-child of Lady Luck! The resale of the rod would catch me a cool $1500. After that I'd go to confession and wipe the slate clean.

Simultaneously, he got into his car, started his engine, and reached for the rod case in the back seat. The $50 bill in my wallet had turned blue with age. The dead president on it appeared to have a glint of a smile like he was glad to see air and sunlight. I forked it over to him and received the rod case. I didn't figure the guy to be a law-breaker but he sped out of the lot at NASCAR speed. I uncased the rod patiently expecting my senses to be engulfed in the perfumed fragrances of old world varnish and fishing trips from long ago. Speechless and dumbfounded, I stood there holding a Japanese fly rod.

# Send Lawyers, Guns, and Money

Dateline San Francisco. Late last week San Francisco police were dispatched to the Angler's Lodge in Golden Gate Park to quell an attempted hanging. The necktie party centered on Fred Fishstick who had sold "genuine jungle cock capes" (a rare & endangered species) to GGACC members.

Subsequent investigation by U.S. Customs officials revealed that the capes were made of synthetic materials and traced to a theft that occurred last winter at the International Sportsman's Exhibition in San Mateo.

Fishstick, booked for theft and out on bail, had responded back to the Angler's Lodge to collect monies owed him. Apparently his mere presence promulgated a disturbance that quickly escalated to a small riot and ultimately a rebellion that led to his near fatal hanging. He is presently in police custody at San Francisco General for rope burns and broken bones; he is expected to be rebooked for the additional charge of inciting a riot.

Uncle Al Fresco
c/o Angler's Lodge
Golden Gate Park
San Francisco

Dear Al,

I would have written long before this had my health permitted. Al, the wolf's at my door, and worse he's got a hold of my leg.

I think you know me well enough Al, a sincere and honorable Joe, financially secure and all about self-respect. And this is why I find it regrettable and unfortunate to write you that I'm a little light this winter and could use a helping hand.

Financial legalities and allegations stemming from my importing business are the root cause of my temporary setback.

Al, I know I can count on you for lawyers, guns, and money if need be. You're that kind of person. So, if you would, please be kind enough to drop a little loot in a letter and forward it to me.

By the way, this loan will be repaid almost immediately. I've received word from the Publisher's Clearing House folks that I'm a bona fide guaranteed finalist in their contest—so look for my return check rather quickly in the mail.

Yours for truth,

Freddie Fishstick
c/o San Francisco General Hospital

# You Know Me Al

Dear Al,

The only X-mas card I received this year was hand delivered by a process server. It was from my ex-wife. Holiday carols? I got one of those too: "Silent Night," compliments of PG&E. They turned off my power. On the plus side, I have a "semi-job-offer" at an all-night pancake house as an Assistant Manager Trainee. They said they'd get back to me.

Hey you know me Al, roll with the punches, play out those hunches—I went fishing. East Creek, a feeder stream to the Pit River in the Warner Mountains with butter-colored browns and redband rainbows seemed in order. On the way up, I stopped in Reno and made a few short-term investments. With what little I had left, I fortified myself at Bob's Big Boy buffet (for the heavy eater). After a memorable meal, a thought occurred to me. I gotta stop pushing myself the way I do, so I took a room at the Rendezvous Motel. Outside of Tijuana and the Rendezvous Motel in Reno, $19.95 motel rooms are in short supply. Talk about amenities Al, you can lie in bed and shave. The rooms have mirrored ceilings.

Daybreak found me driving up highway 395 towards Alturas. I took a side trip through the Skedaddle Mountains for no other reason than I liked the name. I turned right at Likely and stopped at the general store. A big orange sign said "Deer Hunters Welcome." The old gent behind the counter said the archery deer season was opening tomorrow as I purchased 6 locally tied "Killer" flies. The old boy said, "When you tie these on, make sure you're away from the stream, preferably behind a rock or tree—cause the trout'll be jumping out atcha like Barracudas. No Joke, bettern' live bait."

Four miles in on the county road, a cardboard sign read "Road Closed," and ten miles in was another which read "Can't You Read It's Closed." The signs were primitively made and appeared unofficial.

I arrived at Blue Creek campground near nightfall. To my far left was an old green pickup with a rifle rack and an old yeller dog lying in the back. Four shade tree mechanics were under the hood. I pulled to the far right and my tires began crunching over oceans of apples and cow salt licks. Did a truck tip over and spill its contents, or was there "deer baiting" going on?

As I set camp, the welcoming committee joined me. The Modoc County Sheriff's Office (I went there later to file a vandalism to my vehicle report) told me that the crew sounded like the Burns brothers, Side and Rug, and their two cousins, Isaac and Gabby Hayes. All appeared to have questionable bathing habits. One told me they were "wildlife experts" doing research and that the campground was closed. Another concurred and stated that they were doing "scientific studies" on the deer population, and time permitting "might take one honestly" as the opener was tomorrow. "Great," I told them, "but I'm staying." I used my best Bobby De Niro attitude on them. They left. On into the evening I hatched a plan to save the deer and provide a little entertainment to the gang. Fifty Watts of Haggard crooned through the campground that night and into the morning. Hag sang of mama, papa, prison, shep, cheatin, drinkin, and prison as I sawed wood.

I was on the purling waters of East Creek before dawn. Had I kept all the trout caught that morning, I would have had the makings of a nice tin of sardines. Mid-morning made me think of some good grub for breakfast so I eased on back towards camp. Al, Robin Hood would have been proud of the arrows whistling in, around, and through the campground.

As I entered the campground a sudden frost seemed to fall onto the campground and all activity stopped.

My pickup truck and camper had been "shot up" with arrows.

Al, you know me. No more Mr. Nice Guy, the gloves were coming off. Three of the four started running for the hills as I stormed into their campground. I caught the fourth coming out of the outhouse pants down and pinned him up against his truck. I wanted the facts. Pronto.

What he lacked in truthfulness he made up in originality. "Beats me son but it looks to me like you been attacked by Indians," he replied.

I've given up on fishing. I joined a mid-winter bowling league and can be reached at,

> Freddie Fishstick
> C/O Midtown Bowl
> San Francisco, Calif.

# No Bright Lights, No Big City

When one retires, moving from a big city to a small town seems to be right up an elder's alley. Big blue skies, song birds, and a sweet slow life beside a river. He and his wife thought so too, and moved north to a hamlet of 500 or so beside the Sacramento River in Northern California. Cowlusa. The motto written below the city limit sign identified the town as the "Home of the Battling Bluegill." A fishing friend mentioned to him that the area he was moving to was five miles past the end of the earth. They brought a lot of their furniture with them. He brought a lot of excess baggage too—his mind.

It's safe to say that the Sacramento River has nothing in common with the Old Suwanee. He watched the river on sunny summer days as a healthy supply of alcoholics and speed crazed lunatics on speed boats, ski boats, and other out-of-control water craft whirled the waters like Osterizers. Some folks would think that fall and winter would bring tranquil times back to river. Well the river wasn't having it. He thought that it was pissed off for being disrespected and it rose and raised hell. It busted its banks, flooded, and winnowed through the river valley with biblical forces. He bought a canoe and placed it beside his bedroom window, just in case.

His wife's idea of socializing on holidays with family began and ended on their first Thanksgiving up there. It was a doozy. He came from a long line of boozers and basket cases, and it was never more evident than that night. He'd had a snootful, a family tradition. His teetotaling mother-in-law asked him what he thought of "us country folks?" and he opened up with the goodness of the farmers around those parts. "Like Old MacDonald and his farm only better." He said he had witnessed many acts of kindness, for instance, "helping barnyard animals over fences, mostly sheep." He took another strong snort from his wine glass and added that the history of their area could be easily linked to the phone book, in that most folks had the same last names. He said that it appeared that some inbreeding had taken place as more than one person bore a passing resemblance to Mortimer Snerd, the buck toothed puppet.

One spring weekend he invited some of his buddies from the city up for a fishing trip, at the State Park campground on the river. Once they were there, he drove them through the two block downtown area. Then he backed up and showed it to them again so they could relive the past.

That weekend the town went dry. Lonnie's Liquor, Lottery and Live Bait Shop was set on fire by no one other than Lonnie. He cracked. The cops showed up first, clubbed him, and carried him off while he screamed "How the hell do I know what they're biting on?" The town's volunteer fire department broke out and formed a bucket brigade from the river to the liquor store. No dice. The building looked like a burnt tortilla.

Civic resolve showed up that night as town folk stormed City Hall and demanded that the permit process be bypassed and that a new building be erected without delay. Also, a movement was afoot, almost immediately, to get a new fire truck.

Our friend from the city read in the paper that the Woman's Guild was going to have a fund raiser, an ice cream social at the library. Weeks later he would read that it flopped like a three scoop snow cone. Next, the Sacramento Quilting Society held a Quilt Fair at the Grange Hall, also without much success.

The boys down at Sporty's Tavern had a better idea. They'd hold a Homebrew and Distillation Symposium at the Veteran's Hall. Tickets sold out fast, and a walk up crowd was anticipated. The city fathers required that a rent-a-cop be on the premises. By mid-morning the three man police department was summoned for crowd control. By noon, mutual aid from the highway patrol was requested, and by nightfall the National Guard from Sacramento was on the scene.

A week later, the *Voice of the Valley* newspaper featured a photo of the city fathers beside a brand new (to them) second hand 50 gallon pumper.

Incidentally, that week's edition also featured another interesting article on "Hooliganism at the State Park." There was a photo of a ranger pointing to a large hole that appeared to have been hit by a meteor. The ranger said that the hole had formerly been a campsite and pointed to discarded liquor bottles, beer cans (not high quality stuff he added) and the remnants of what could have been a Coleman Stove in another life, before the explosion. He said that a "gang" from the city was responsible for this mayhem. Further, he went on to say that one in the group was apprehended running from an adjacent campsite with an armload of stolen fishing gear and later claimed that he suffered from a sleepwalking disorder. Lastly, in the parking lot by the outhouse, one of the gang woke up what few campers were left by yelling hysterically, "Snake! Snake!" as he stomped a fan belt into submission.

Well, having taken all that he could take up there in that small town, he put his house up for sale. He and she would be moving back to the city. The house was put on the market the day the market crashed two years ago. In the meantime, he is back on his couch, the one with springs so weak his ass hits the ground, and waiting for an old dream to occur, the one where aliens abduct him for a second time in the same week.

# Columbus Day

Every October a huge wave of humanity gathers force and breaks over the streets of San Francisco like a tsunami. On one particular weekend there is usually a 49ers football game, the U.S. Navy Fleet Week, the Blue Angels air show, perhaps even a Giants baseball game, and tourists up the wazoo.

He of course was in the city for another reason, a grammar school reunion for St. Elizabeth's Grammar School, which he and his former classmates referred to as Lizzie's Prison. Time permitting, he planned a trip into Italian Town, North Beach, to visit old friends, talk about the old times, and create some new ones.

It's safe to say that his grammar school was the elephant burial ground of potential scholars. Accomplishments were never mentioned at the yearly function. There were none. The words moocher, swindler and wino would not be too far off from a description of his classmates. The reunion always seemed to end early and was a repeat of the year before, with maybe a new story or two, or a fellow student reminiscing about the first handgun he bought from an 8th grader.

When he left the reunion he drove over to Slim's Bait Shop to shoot the shit with Slim. In the neighborhood parlance Slim was "a good guy to know," not so much for fishing information or bait, but for racing forms, liquor, and for fencing stolen property. Slim often quoted himself, "In my business, information, and lack of information comes at a price" as if it were the 11th commandment.

There were two benches on each side of the bait shop and the old *paisanos* powwowed there daily, smoking cheap Tuscano stogies, drinking cheap red wine and waiting for a story to start. To the best of his recollection these boys have been kibitzing on those benches since way before cell phones, satellite dishes, possibly even before fire, and since back when folks were memorizing Latin verbs. They called themselves the Bacala Boys after a no account cod back in Italy.

Slim came out first and mentioned that the 25-cent-a-cup honor system coffee mess was being closed until further notice. There appeared to be a major discrepancy between the receipts and the amount of coffee consumed. That matter concluded without comment.

Primo brought up his fishing trip to Mexico the weekend before. At the Aeropuerto de La Paz he mentioned to some boys at the bar that he was an apostle of traveling light with his fishing gear. Apparently one listener took him at his word and swiped his fishing rods.

Big Tony chimed in with a high country story. He claimed that the mosquitoes (*Alpini colossi*) were so big in Alpine County that they voted in the last presidential election. This raised a few eyebrows, and he quickly recanted, advising that a few had been seen canvassing the voting booths. He took it up a notch after that though and made mention of an article in last summer's *Markleeville Register* that said that two large mosquitoes had carried off a woman's poodle, and apparently not satisfied, came back for her. He said he could produce the newspaper article but it would take a while for him to locate it.

Guido mentioned the morning the fog socked in the muni pier last summer when he single handedly fought the fish of a lifetime for over two hours. When the fog lifted it revealed an angry swimmer from the Dolphin Swim Club. Guido had snagged him in the ass. The swimmer roughed Guido up pretty good. Guido had no idea that fishing was such a violent sport.

"Did he take out much line?" Primo asked.

Dante mentioned last summer's trout trip on the Merced River in Yosemite. He threw a prodigious cast across a canoe eating rapid that inadvertently latched onto the rear bumper of a passing Greyhound bus. He said the bus was solidly hooked and that "the fight was on." Briefly. He concluded by adding that had he had a larger fishing reel the outcome would have been different. He validated his story with fine flight of fancy—"The bus had just left the Ahwahnee Hotel headed downhill to Modesto with a full head of steam."

Primo stood up and stretched, and said that he had just perfected a new way to fish. With his new method you could reach over all ocean breakers and obstructions with ease. You attach your lure or bait to a bottle rocket and ignite it, no need to cast. He veered off and said he was waiting on one last governmental agency's approval. "Who?" they asked. "NASA" he replied.

Sal said that the boys were missing the point on this particular weekend and requested a moment of reverence on this holiest of holidays—Columbus Day, the day that Christopher discovered America, and more importantly, the tomato and brought it back to Italy. By all accounts, this discovery proved to be the perfect marriage to Marco Polo's noodle escapade in China. Two of the boys closed their eyes and made the sign of the cross. They raised their wine glasses and issued a strong "Salute!" for pastaciutta.

"Don't forget to mention meatballs," Guido added.

The fog horns croaked near the Golden Gate Bridge as *Las Barcas*, the boats, or what may have been boats commenced to promenade between the two bridge towers and into the Bay before the day's highlight, the Blue Angels air show. Visibility was in short supply. You could hear diesel engines, and see enormous wakes rise and recede on the shoreline, but you really couldn't quite tell what kind of boats were out there. In the past and on a clear day, you could expect to see San Francisco Fire Department boats shooting a steady stream of water and preceding the U.S. Navy warships past the pier. Weather permitting, a flotilla of smaller sailboats, skiffs and shrimp boats followed the big ships astern, like a flock of seagulls. Today was different. What steamed by the shoreline was anybody's guess.

The gang from the bait shop got up, stretched, and started walking down Columbus Avenue through the Italian street *festa* towards the piers to catch the action. The scent of marinated garlic swirled with fragrant stromboli, spaghetti sugo, and heavy helping of Frank and Dino singing Italian traditionals over the loudspeakers. The group strutted through the fair like grand marshals. They stopped once, and only once, and bowed their heads in stony silence when their national anthem played—the theme from *The Godfather*.

They took their customary spots at the edge of the muni pier and waited two hours for the Blue Angels air show. They could have waited a lot longer with the same results. The air show was cancelled due to inclement conditions.

# San Francisco Banking

There is nothing speculative about the city's Automatic Teller Machines (ATMs). A short stroll down Montgomery Street puts you in a place where it is possible to transact banking business worldwide on a single city block. Words pertaining to "maybe," "possibly" or "perhaps" are incongruent to any transaction. It's always automatic.

One hundred and forty-eight miles north of the Bay Bridge lies a trout stream that can easily be described as weekend water. Years ago when we discovered the stream it was a hard dollar to fish. There was simply way too much water to wade, and very small concentrations of unconcerned fish.

Through misfortunes, mishaps, and blind luck our gang agreed that the stream could best be fished by separating it into two sections: an upper run, and a lower run of comparable length. The upper run pinches through granite and requires up and down mountaineering to maintain streamside presence. The lower run allows you stroll beside the stream and listen to its dream song. It's easy on your eyes and ears.

The two runs are separated by one large and all but impassable chasm overarched by boulders the size of buildings. The water is very deep and very cold. Ingress and egress in either direction requires swimming or scaling a mountainside. There is nothing to remind you of Grahame's gentle *Wind in the Willows* river ride. There is a Toad Hall there though, and you'll be greeted with a quick alarming croak while you watch Mr. Toad mad dash downstream on his wild ride through the white water below. Amazingly enough, no one that we know of has ever caught a trout in that pool, and yet, when you see it, you're stunned. It's equal to anything the deep blue sea has to offer, and easily recognizable as the beating heart of this watershed. The pool is called "the Gates."

There are three pools perched just beneath the Gates that are as reliable as any ATM on earth. That said, early spring signals an early run on these pools/ATMs when the bait boys appear, and disappear just as quickly.

The holes are labeled Wells Fargo, Washington Mutual, and Bank of America. Deposit a well placed fly and your transaction begins. You'll need Lady Luck on your side to land one. These trout dip, dart, and jump like jet fighters.

The lowest of the three pools is called the Wells Fargo Pool. There is an extraordinarily high red bluff that shades the stream flow during every minute of daylight. A small bead head nymph is your pin number. Insert this outfit into the white water just above the pool, let it follow the bubble line through the pool, and it's "Katy bar the door" because more than likely the fish you hook, not land, will do everything possible to abort the transaction. Let the pool rest well, and repeat the transaction.

A hundred yards up from the Wells Pool the stream rejoins itself after a half mile split. Two currents collide with each other and form the Washington Mutual (WaMu) pool. You have no idea how good your good luck is going to be. A waterborne Blue Angel bends and banks on your dry fly, and probably eludes you too. An irrepressible beaver dam rests squarely in center. This is a one shot deal. No second chances. Only one withdrawal per day.

On the high end of the run, just below the Gates pool, rests the Bank of America (BofA) hole. So noted as the oldest and most prolific pool on the stream, as is the Montgomery Street BofA. It's midway up the creek, and leisurely lunches rule. Someone in our group conducts business as we sit stream side and swap stories. It's a common courtesy to allow others to tell their tales first. Then of course you can exaggerate on their exaggerations. An unsolicited "Whoo hoo!" usually interrupts our gabfest and signals your turn at the ATM. The angler who has hooked the fish either lands it, or winds up sobbing and sighing. Either way, it's another's turn.

As in any financial or fish market, there are ups and downs. We have a pool for just those occasions. We fish it with serendipity and capriciousness. We christened it after a colleague long since gone. His name was Charles Upson. The pool is affectionately titled "Upsons' Downs."

He was a banker.

# *Watercolors*

There are some city people who need noise. He is not one of them. He likes straight lines, solid colors, and silence.

There is a forced movement of the city that makes him crack. Escalators, elevators, watching a world through glass, breathing air in compartments, those kinds of things, that secretly, and very completely, make him go to pieces. At one point, fairly recently, he had been talked back off the ledge by the authorities.

Herding mentality and urbanity always made him recede, like a low tide clam, to lower, slower and deeper environs, like the San Francisco Public Library. It seemed to be some sort of a silent salvation for him.

There, he can hear himself think a thought, clearly, and quietly. Mentally, he made concessions a long time ago to modernity in library matters. The 3" by 5" cards analogous to oak drawers and the Dewey Decimal System had given way to a robot that cranked out titles and authors quicker than a finger snap. The hand-written, hand-stamped library card was now something akin to a Visa card, or a driver's license, with a metal strip on its backside. Electronic doors.

He felt at home in the library. He was constantly searching for photographs of water, moving water, watercolors, unfamiliar fish and their environs, and things like that.

It's always the same to him, spring water, tidewater, gutter water as long as it is moving. Somewhere. There is always a euphoric feeling within him, near his heart. He thinks it may be a medical condition.

One glossy periodical holds the greatest influence over him: *Field & Stream*, and its water color photographs. It's his Bible, the library is his church, and he attends services regularly, right after the monthly edition arrives.

*Field & Stream*, the nation's earliest sporting publication, is his Ecclesiastes, the Old Testament. For sure there are other periodicals, *Outdoor Life*, and *Sports Afield* to name two. *Field & Stream* is something special though. It cuts up the country like cordwood; the civilized Eastern Seaboard, a very southern South, the Midwest and the Wild West are sectionalized. Each region has its own field editor, a rod and reel guy, and an outdoorsman who takes to water like a duck.

Its eastern watercolor photos always throw him a curve. The creeks back there are clear. Translucent. Fragile, flawless, and free of impurities. It seemed as though you would never be in water over your head, and if you were, you would still be able to see clearly. The trout are cut from the same cloth as their streams. Dainty is not too small a word to describe them. "Eastern Brook Trout" they're called, and just about as charming a fish as the chaps who fished for them. When it came to color, these fish were Technicolor.

Those southern stream photos, oh those southern streams are a horse of a different color. Many green colors: asparagus, chartreuse, moss, and olive. But certainly no shamrock. Sludge and slow-moving currents come to mind. The fish down there, mostly bass, appeared to be part chameleon, in that their colors reflected, if it seems possible, greener green hues to completely camouflage their being.

Midwestern watercolor photos, all their waterways had the same theme, certain shades of brown. The lakes look like Earl Grey tea, the streams diffuse blends of rust, copper, and wheat. Their fish don't take a back seat to anyone either, they're real dillies, muskellunge, northern pike, walleyes and pickerel. These fish have two things in common, size and teeth, and judging from these photographs, they know how to use them. In a fish fight, a piranha would swim for his life.

Way out west the streams seemed silver. Everywhere, every kind of water had this coinage palette perfected. Ansel Adams printed his photographs using a silver gelatin method. To him, *Field & Stream's* photos were silver medals, second place. Silver, the sometimes by-product of gold, copper and zinc was a match made in heaven for a blue-tinted trout or a high-seas salmon. The permeated spectrum of silver on dark denim, azure, aquamarine, or Dodger blue is to him, well, royal.

To be truthful, he picks up a *National Geographic* every now and then. He shows a minor interest in ice; a glacier, an iceberg, maybe a snow-capped mountain. The thing is, it fails to move him, not like moving water and watercolors.

# Whitecaps on a Creek

*"Remember to get the weather in your god damned book—weather is very important."*
—Hemingway

Every time we venture towards a fly or bait shop to purchase some superfluous article, it seems as though the impulse is driven by part of a dream, a vision, or a bad piece of advice. These angling "breakthroughs" are always part of a mindless mental floss that foresees a future date with destiny when everything works.

Perhaps. In retrospect, we are usually the victims of what advertising does best: Lie. Angling journals and televised programs paint pictures of a sunny-ray day and a contented crowd, with a full creel for our fishing fraternity.

The reality of that world has nothing in common with our dreamscapes. We're San Franciscans.

Way out there, behind every mild morning fogbank is the real San Francisco treat. It has nothing to do with Rice-a-Roni, and everything to do with afternoon wind-chopped waters that send every angler we've ever known flying towards the great indoors.

Mr. San Francisco, the *Chronicle's* Herb Caen, once described San Francisco as living inside a great grey pearl. He wasn't far off.

When dawn draws near our coastline we're greeted with unruffled waters, low lying clouds (fog), and some sort of minor-league drizzle from above. In the not so long ago, west of Twin Peaks drivers used their windshield wipers daily, kids played outdoors wearing rubber yellow raincoats, and every now and then police took a report of a child being "lost" in the fog while playing on their front lawn. Just another summer day in the city. The rest of the city was luckier, there was always fog overhead, only higher.

By midmorning, the sun, like a very low-wattage light bulb, breaks through the haze on our western shoreline and anglers appear. They're the smart set. They've been there since long before dawn.

Out at Ocean Beach the striped bass boys are flinging lures unfathomable distances. Some Golden Gate Fleet party boat skippers are busy bouncing bait for bottom fish just south of the city. Others are north of the Potato Patch Shoal near the Marin County headlands snooping for salmon.

Just past the jackals and hyenas at the San Francisco Zoo lies fogbound Lake Merced, known locally as "Lake Mistake," principally because of the abominable action inflicted on it by its most ardent admirers: us, and our own particular brand of self serving love. The gang out there wets lines for trout. Bayside, people are positioned on piers crabbing, or trying to catch a decent-sized perch. Out on the Bay, boats are drifting for halibut and sharks.

Near noon, the fog has vaporized. Newcomers are lured outside by this lull, or break in the weather. Unwittingly, we proceed outside for picnics and other outdoor pursuits, most arriving at the beginning of the sunshine ending.

The second part our sonata starts in the form of a light wisp of wind. All boats at sea, and all anglers on shore look westward. Our star-crossed sea has begun its crescendo. Shore flags start to flutter and banner masts out at sea begin to ripple. It's always near 2:00 p.m. when white foam forms on wave tops, and most boaters start to head home, full steam ahead, towards safe harbors. The first zephyr zooms in around 3:00, and the shore-bound clan start reeling in and running to their cars. By 4:00, a full force gale is in progress. All our anglers are ashore and inside, wind-burned and weak. Small craft warnings are as common as crows out here. If San Francisco had a creek of any consequence, it would have white caps on it by 5:00 p.m.

Near nightfall the west wind has blown itself to bits. Caen's great grey pearl, the fog, has enveloped the city. In the morning, our enduring climatic circle will repeat itself again.

Our angling attire out here consists of down jackets and hooded sweatshirts. Some say a snowmobile suit is just as applicable. There is not a tourist alive in the city that does not have our hearts. We see them shivering in polo shirts, shorts, and sandals every summer. Others can be seen with white loafers, socks, and a matching patent leather belt. We affectionately call that style of dress "The Full Cleveland." And for their own sake, we always hope that they don't go fishing.

# An Insignificant Salmon

They used to be everywhere around here—the small ladder of streams from Santa Cruz to San Francisco, the creeks just north of the Golden Gate Bridge on up to the Klamath River, and inside the Bay—in some of the most improbable trickles on earth.

They were second cousins to the steelhead, and acrobats as well. They were the first to appear on the surf line that preceded any estuary or creek ingress. It was always in the fall, late fall.

They were called Coho, or silver salmon because they were. It was no big deal to land a limit of these fish. Out on the big briny, party boat skippers sheepishly filled out with light limits of these small salmon, or, if no one noticed, "released" the smaller ones to an unfathomable fate. The unbridled commercial gang got in on the act too. They used drag nets to do their damage, and dropped the very dead, undersized ones overboard. The silvers were "heading south" just like the sardines, dwindling away, like the Dodo did.

The Department of Fish and Game seemed disinterested. All salmon hatcheries in California are rigged for Kings, and some small slots were saved for steelhead, the glamour guys in this bunch. A salmon like the silver, which may mature at 2 pounds, was apparently of insufficient interest to the boys in Sacramento.

Oddly enough, our local strain was a super strain. In 1959, a 22-pounder was caught at Papermill Creek, in Marin County, just across the bridge from the city. It was a world record at that time. By no means is this an insignificant fish or feat. Silvers inhabit creeks clear up to Alaska and across the Bearing Strait into Russia.

A book co-authored by the California Department of Fish and Game, the California Academy of Sciences, and the Sierra Club entitled *California's Wild Heritage: Threatened and Endangered Animals in the Golden State* lists lots of fish as being up against it. Twenty-eight to be exact. It surprised us locals. The Shortnose Sucker, the Colorado Squawfish, and those darlings of the desert, the Pupfish, all merited a page in this publication. The super-small silver salmon did not make the cut. They were listed as a "Species of Special Concern" on the last page of this publication, with no other notation.

It may be said that this freewheeling little salmon was his own worst enemy in that he rarely refused anything thrown his way out on the high seas, and it is true that that logging and sedimentation have crushed every creek along the coastline to some degree. But we should also take a solid look at ourselves. It was not too many years ago that we allowed trout fishing in our coastal creeks, and the limit was 10, then 5, then none. These coastal streams are now closed to all angling. More young-of-the-year silvers were creeled as "trout" than trout on the opening day of the "trout season." If they had closed the creeks sooner, or if an observant angler had taken the time to differentiate between the forked tail of a silver and the square tail of a trout, perhaps they may have lasted longer, and in larger numbers.

Human nature, and mother nature, are hard acts to gauge. That super strain of silvers in Papermill Creek was stymied as much by Nicasio Dam as by those folks who built luxury homes and golf courses across the entire San Geronimo Valley. The silvers had no idea what they were dealing with—they kept coming. So very few that they were unrecognizable to all, excluding the enlightened eye of anglers and conservationist who took it upon themselves to clean up the creek and increase the habitat, and hopefully, the future homes of these fish.

As of late, their numbers are increasing in this watershed and elsewhere. Others are taking note and following this creek's lead. Down on the San Lorenzo River and along Pescadero Creek south of the city, incremental numbers of silvers are on the rise. North of the city, and way on up in Mendocino County, wildlife managers and watershed keepers are using silvers as environmental totems, somewhat like canaries in mine shafts. Inside the Bay, steelhead are swimming through Stanford, by way of San Francisquito Creek. Across the Bay, over on Alameda Creek, these same fish are hand-lifted over BART structures so that they can continue on to their Sunol Valley spawning grounds. These efforts are not insignificant. It's not to late for the silvers, anywhere. We've learned that much.

# A Toxic River Will Run Through It

*I write this with great respect for the four families
that actually reside on the Cortina Rancheria.*

Apanolio Creek flows west beneath Ox Mountain on the Coast Range. After its confluence with Pillarcitos Creek, it glides towards the Pacific Ocean through the town of Half Moon Bay, five miles distant.

The First Nation people, the Coastanoans and Pomos, coexisted peacefully with the Apanolio watershed since who knows when. Spanish explorers and the blessings of self-promoting missionary priests took care of that. But during the next 250 years of development the creek still held its own. Self-sustaining populations of salmon and steelhead, shellfish, upland birds, small mammals, and sea birds held on. Mother Nature is nothing but resilient.

Human nature, always a tough thing to gauge, changed that. The powers that be in San Mateo County graciously allowed a waste management company—read "garbage and dump" company—to secure the headwaters of this creek with accepted best practices and EPA approval. Best practices included a base of clay, waste matter, another base of clay and so on, until the creek canyon was filled. The dump was named "The Ox Mountain Sanitary Landfill," and it was anything but sanitary.

Mitigation factors included a series of sedimentation dams below the dump site (Apanolio Creek) that theoretically stopped toxic leachate from breeching into the creek. The leachate material was trucked to Kesterson in the San Joaquin basin. The Kesterson site was closed down in the early 1980s by the federal government. Extraordinary amounts of livestock and wildlife deformities were traced to selenium to the basin. The basin is now closed and declared a toxic waste site.

The sedimentation dams on Apanolio Creek collapsed in 1992 and much of the wildlife, and all the fish went with them. On any given day a count of 60 to 80 dead seagulls with fungal parasites were in evidence, and traces of *E. coli* bacteria exist in the surviving birds to this day. Parts of the creek that had held self-sustaining potable water still remain non-potable. The dump closes in 2027.

Some time ago, down in New Mexico, the government tested atomic bombs in the desert near White Plains. That was over 60 years ago. The residual radiation effect on the human population and their lands never ended. These people are now referred to in government circles as the affected and infected "down wind" people.

It's safe to say that our south county cousins in Colusa County will be inadvertently subjected to this same scenario without full knowledge aforethought.

History is apparently a low hurdle, in that Cortina Creek is a mirror image of the Apanolio landfill project, but worse. A system of methane gas releases will have to be put in place to release and burn the gasses that will form eternally from inside the landfill. Flames can and will erupt from the landfill and spew into an airborne stench. The seagulls, songbirds, and upland game that enter the creek drainage will not confine their flights solely to this watershed. Their effluents will be dispersed on the winds, water and landscape of this county and valley in an unimaginable environmental hell.

There are four First Nation families who reside on Cortina Creek, only four families, and some have voiced strong opposition to the project. The power to move forward rests in the hands of 275 distant "Instant Indians" who by virtue of their blood have a vote in favor of the project.

Lessons not learned at Kesterson and on Apanolio Creek repeat themselves, leaving scars on winds, waters and landscapes that won't heal.

When winter's rains fall on Cortina Creek, the falling water just might be the tears of First Nation forefathers who watch their sons render their lands useless for the highest sum.

Mother Nature is no match for the greed of human nature.

Roll over Rachel Carson, please tell Colusa County the news.

# Swimming with Summer Runs

Below a blue mountain and alongside a green stream we dropped our backpacks. Hansel and Gretel would have liked the small meadow. Bob, a State game warden, and I had roughed it all day. It was time to smooth out the evening. We drank like hillbillies. Our campfire burnt well, and in some sense more truly; if there's a campfire, there's a story.

It was late last spring. People were starting to move; new lessons were beginning. I was to assist Bob on a stream census of summer run steelhead in the Yolla Bolly-Middle Eel Wilderness.

From George's Valley Trailhead we would follow a 13-mile trail up, over and down a sawtooth ridge to the Balm of the Gilead. The Balm holds the largest concentration of summer runs in the Eel River drainage, and quite possibly in California. Headwatered beneath Vinegar Peak, the Balm begins as a treacherous reach of water that settles down agreeably to navigable runs, and glides in the 4-mile census stretch.

The summer runs ascend the creek on slate gray torrents from the Middle Eel. The Eel River was, and is one of Northern California's more fabled part-time rivers.

That first morning streamside I was religious. I'm always that way when I have a hangover. I told myself I'd drink again when the moon turned blue.

Bob wetsuited and slipped into that first pool as easily as a seal in an aquarium. I unwetsuited and porpoised in and out. Hypothermia is not my idea of a good time. Penguins would have been happy in that creek. Shivering, quivering, I sat on a rock and waited for my usual confidence (which was none) to build back up. It occurred to me that moving water and meditation are wedded forever. I eased into a good old-fashioned snooze while I meditated, and woke up on a particularly large snort.

Extraordinary wouldn't be too large of a word to describe it. Slanted rays of light filtered into the canyon and into my hide. Two swifts were working a warm little wind, an ouzel on the dole cascaded from rock to rock. A pair of wind-up chipmunks studied me curiously, much like a high school science class's first observance of a platypus. As I drank in the overture of this splendid spring morning, a rifle shot voice pierced the stillness. "Hey! Get your head out of you're a__, there's work to be done!" Enough said.

Without too much difficulty, I dog paddled towards the high-banked side of the pool. Alders and ferns bunched together on the bank. I descended into the deep recesses of the creek. Facing upstream, in what appeared to be a hypnotic trance, were five steelhead. Although partially obscured by tree roots, rock outcroppings and ferns, the unmistakable gunbarrel blue backs with flanked silver sides were in evidence. I surfaced and went to shore.

It really wasn't what I saw that day that mattered, but what I felt, and it came from the deepest part of me. For one to look too closely at these summer runs is to pull them apart like flowers. I withdrew with reverence. Alighting from pool to pool, sunlight to shadow, Bob and I leapfrogged to the confluence of the Balm with the Eel. We counted 181 fish, some over 10 lbs.

Nightfall, near a pool of moonlight, our fire embered and we reflected on the day's work. There would be no requiem for the Balm. The congenital thirst of an urbanizing north state, sea lions, logging, and squawfish had not reduced the Balm's carrying capacity. The renaissance flowered in the form of an adjusted catch and release season for the sporting angler.

# Feather River Rising

The coastline is always clear in late September, when an apricot-colored sun commonly slips beneath the Pacific horizon. Schools of salmon breach the Golden Gate on an incoming flood tide and hug the Marin County shoreline, finning north. At the old California City net depot near Tiburon, the fish cordwood up and wait for an outgoing ebb tide.

River waters from the great valley streams press through Carquinez Strait down through San Pablo Bay, around Point San Pablo and on into San Francisco Bay. The onrushing waters cross the Bay at this point, and proceed full speed ahead towards California City. The salmon's olfactory senses kick in and a mad rush across Bay waters ensues. On this singular outgoing tide the salmon breach the Strait, bound for their final glory. In less than three days the salmon run up through the Delta country, slip up into the Sacramento River, and fan out up into its major tributaries.

First Nation Tribes, the river valley's Wintun, came to call their running waters Bohema-mem, "great water" or Nom-Tee-Mem, "over the hill water." Early Spanish explorers, with an ecumenical blessing from the padres, would re-christen these waters "Sacramento," the blessed sacrament, after an ecclesiastical belief.

The tributary of the Sacramento with the greatest volume would become "El Rio de las Plumas"—the river of feathers. An exploratory party noted a field of springtime dandelions bursting airborne near the river and remarked on their resemblance to feathers.

The Feather River and its forks suffered an unfathomable fate. Twenty-two dams and eleven powerhouses harnessed its strength and it became touted as the Pacific Gas and Electric Company's "Staircase of Power."

A fish ladderless river was no good to anyone, and with the world's largest earth filled dam in place at Oroville, a fish hatchery at the base of the dam was formulated to augment a ghost run of fish that exists only in the minds, hearts and souls of old-time anglers.

The Oroville Dam project was sold as a recreational project for the masses. In reality, the project was the cornerstone of the Central Valley Project that diverted water through the Delta, and down to Southern California. Below the dam are two additional reservoirs, the forebay, and the afterbay. Some say that these bays were created for recreation, others advise that this water storage is a reclamation afterthought. Water is released at a precise time and temperature for farmland production below. Either way, the water diverted into the two bays reduces the river to a lower flow, and, in turn, conceived four miles of the most productive salmon and steelhead riffle water in California. These days, it has come to be called the "low flow" section of the Feather River.

The state fish hatchery at Oroville, just above the low flow section, raises and releases two million salmon fingerlings and ten thousand sub-catchable steelhead each year. The salmon are released at Crockett near Carquinez Strait. The steelhead are released at Grimes, 18 miles below the hatchery. Twenty percent of the salmonids caught off the coast are of Feather River origin.

The Oroville State Wildlife area encloses both sides of the riffle water and roads parallel the entire west side, and some of the east side. Islands braid the river into smaller rivulets making wading a breeze. Another favored method is a leisurely float on any watercraft. A boat, a barn door, or an inner tube will suffice. If you feel that you are into water over your head, stand up; it's that shallow. The put-in is behind McGrath's Bait and Tackle at the start of the low flow section. The take-out is at the afterbay. McGrath's will run your vehicle down river to the take-out for $20.00. The Chico Fly Shop and McGrath's provide alternative guide services.

The favorite time of year for fly fishermen is early fall, and the preferred fly is a pale salmon egg imitation with a nymph trailer. This rig is placed behind a piece of shot, and below an indicator. The best action almost always comes from the small jack salmon and the their smaller first cousins, the yearling steelhead. Hooking larger salmon always seems to occur. The odds of landing one are slim to none. Most folks break them off before breaking their rods and their spirit.

It's a real pleasant place to be during the most perfect time of year. It's a fall favorite.

# A Deer Creek Diary

Thirty-five years after the Sioux Nations defeated Custer, and twenty-five years after Geronimo's Apaches laid down their Winchesters, North America's last pure Indian surrendered to civilization. He was the last of his kind. The date was August 11th, 1911. The white world would come to know this Indian as "Ishi." For four and a half very short years this gentle native would become the toast of San Francisco, and the principle jewel in the University of California's anthropological crown.

As an 1870 adolescent, Ishi was a member of North California's Yahi Triblet, less than thirty in number. Ishi would witness his band's last five able-bodied males place their bows at the doorstep of a rancher's cabin east of Tehama. It was a betoken of peace. A ranch hand's furtive move frightened the five, and they fled back up into the foothills, and with good reason. "To live, and let live" was not an axiom applicable to the great western movement. The past score of years saw Yahi numbers dwindle as the United States Army's Pacific Command, Governor Leland Stanford's Troopers, Peter Lassen's Vaqueros, trackers, and footloose criminals shot, hung, raped, crippled, maimed, kidnapped and legally indentured their kind.

After the five-bow incident, the Yahis would conceal themselves in the inaccessible reaches of Deer Creek. No longer would they harvest the great Sacramento Valley acorns—daily sustenance for bread, soup or mush. No longer would they gather the black basaltic foothill salt, or willows for their basket weaving culture. Their "village" would consist of a small, well-concealed bent branch house, and a smaller cave beside Deer Creek. By 1908, time, illness and age had reduced their number to four. That same year, a survey party came upon them, and the world's smallest free nation vaporized into the winds.

Today's recreationalist moving about the 41,000 acre Ishi Wilderness will find these foothills much like they were back then. Sweet green springtime clover carpets volcanic crevasses. The clover was a seasonal Yahi soup. The buckeye trees provided superior firewood, and their chestnuts nourishment. Alder was used for building, Juniper for bows, and Hazel for arrows. Obsidian, a shiny black glass of volcanic origin, served as arrowheads. Further up from the foothills, in the Digger Pines, the Yahi removed the soft green edible center of pine cones with relish. The Sugar Pine emitted a sweet white gum-like resin that was chewed like candy. The red-berried madrone was a seasonal gift of thin jam gruel. Yahi stealth provided an occasional rabbit, or a rare deer. At that same time, western man's gunpowder ethics were busy depleting wildlife.

In the end though, it would be for the Yahis, and the singular Ishi, as it always was. The life giving waters of the Deer Creek drainage would see them through. Coming out of the cold "sleeps" of winter into the spring "windmoons," the Yahi could count on the heavy-bodied Chinook salmon to ascend upwards to their ancestral homes. In the fall, another abundance of salmon choked Deer Creek's runs and riffles clear up to *Waganupa* (Mt. Lassen). Fresh, salted, dried and preserved, salmon provided the means for maintaining their lives.

These days down among the boughed pepperwoods at Deer Creek Falls, a springtime angler with attentive observation can catch a quick glimpse of an uncommon spring salmon punching up through the white throated cataracts. Rarer still, and with an imaginative mind, deep inside the heavy cold mist, a slight Yahi, crouched, harpoon in hand, patient, intent, and quickly striking airborne silver.

Please read Theodora Kroeber's full account of *Ishi in Two Worlds*. Season that salt tear that touches your lip with Storer and Usinger's *Sierra Nevada Natural History*.

# South Fork

Deep into November the holdout leaves were falling. Gunnard, Mac, and I were driving slowly on a gravel two track. To our left, mist on the river shrouded the South Fork of the Eel. A brown bear cub caught our headlights and vaporized into the fog. Bear scat and huckleberry vines marked the spot.

We bridged the river on two rusted railroad car flatbeds, and drove two thousand feet straight up and into the clouds. We counted seven large blacktail bucks on the way up, in rut, with that love light in their eyes. My partners each reminisced their summer success on this mountain. I sat and sulked, and pondered how my useless deer tag would taste on a slice of bread.

We were on a turkey hunt. We splintered into the woods and commenced to cluck and call the birds in. On a high ridge I sat and watched Mac skirt a pepperwood stand. A butter yellow bobcat and its smaller offspring cracked back behind Mac and pantomimed him step for step, and stop for stop. Thirty yards later the two bobcats decided to abort their stalk and dropped down into a gulch.

On the mountain top we rendezvoused under clear blue skies. Also clear was the absence of turkeys. It appeared as though oak tree acorns were not enough to hold the birds on the hill. We bailed out the day with the sweetest meat in the forest—Mountain Quail. On the way back down towards the river valley we watched a collie-sized coyote, and two others evaporate into a Douglas fir grove, perhaps the deadly precursors of our jaunt.

Down again on the river we crossed back over the emerald green South Fork. Historic October rains had dropped 18 inches on this watershed. The pool beneath the bridge was alive with Chinook Salmon. Natives. Some silver, some not. We left the car and watched them circling the pool from the riffle back into deep depths. A hundred yards upstream, Indian Creek entered the South Fork. Mac forded the river and walked up along the creek without a trace. He likes small streams. Who don't? He'd report later small fish appeared ready to breach the river gap on the next rising.

Later, back on the riverbank we sat near the riffle and watched barebacked salmon slip up the shallow run. Aluminum-sided Steelhead would be coming around the bend soon.

Late at night, sleepless, I counted 7,681 stars, and two comets. They were our lucky stars. I thanked them all for allowing my friends and me to live on this good earth at this time and place.

Should you find yourself on #101 at the Mendocino-Humboldt county line, take the Piercy turnoff. The old #101 route parallels the South Fork and rejoins the new highway at Hartsook. It's a place that's good for the heart, and soul.

# Blake Riffle

Summer's equinox seems to be a sign for the Klamath River's salmon and steelhead. Waxing fat at sea on krill and kelp-bed crustaceans seems to become less interesting to them as a new cognitive force overtakes these fish. Guided by bearings from the sun, the Earth's Magnetic Field, low frequency sounds and scent, they turn towards a place where the ocean ends and a river begins—the Terwer Valley estuary.

The estuary is less than two miles long, and a half mile wide. At daybreak a cool grey marine sky shrouds the river's edge from Requa upstream to Klamath Glen. There is a strong marine influence that provides a salt tang both in the wind and on the water. The first five river riffles are unobservable in the mist. Think San Francisco in the morning.

At night most salmonids breech the surf line on an incoming tide. Ushered in by high waters and covert skies the salmon seek the deep holes while the steelhead seek the first five riffles.

Midmorning coastal fog lifts, and what you thought were F-111s flying overhead turn out to be a phalanx of jet boat boys beating the river bottom with bait—roe balls for King salmon. On the south side of the river the Yurok Nation ply these waters for their sustenance with a gauntlet of 4" nets. Alder smoke and salmon scents grace the afternoon air. From above, seagulls, pelicans and cormorants crash into McDonald, Waukell, Terwer and Glen Riffles removing grilse and runts. From below, submarine-like seals, and river otters add to the confusion. And lastly, like waste management systems in an urban area, an occasional brown bear is on the river bar to clean up entrails and the environment in general.

Above and away from it all, at the end of Starwein Road, and across the road from a mighty fine Italian restaurant, the river pinches in to form Blake Riffle. Redwoods and coastal oaks cast perennial shadows on the river from the south bank. Fish rest here before their assault on to Ah Pah and up through to Blue Creek.

Until someone builds a better river, its the best riffle California has to offer. Claude Kreider in his 1947 book, *Steelhead*, felt it was the most important fly fishing riffle in California. It is the earliest riffle that can be easily fly fished for steelhead in the state. The action begins in August, with Labor Day weekend being the high water mark, and concludes with the first rainfall. The riffle is 60 miles below the Trinity River, a Klamath tributary, and as such, is a location where both river's steelhead runs converge.

At this point the river can be crossed with care, and there is room to cast in a carefree manner. And the weather, well, only in California can you cast for steelhead in short sleeves and shorts. These fish are larger than the "half-pounder" label. The vast majority (and there are lots of them) are cookie cutter fish, twelve inches to slightly less than two pounds. They are blue-backed fish with silver flanks. What these fish lack in size, they make up in numbers and acrobatics, something like a miniature greatest steelhead show on earth.

The river does not place a premium on long distance casting. A bobber, shot, two flies and a repetitious helicopter spin overhead, and a short drift over and through a white-throated chute should net you some fish. GGACC member and master fly tier Larry Kovi tied a marvelous small set of flies for the river.

River access is free. River bar camping with showers is a steal. Motels and restaurants at Requa are more than reasonable. You should give it consideration as a destination if you are looking for some excellent time on the water.

# Big Two-Fisted River

The charm of angling lies in the imminence of surprise. May I kindly add to that, a good book also?

Hemmingway maintained that "All great American literature began and ended with Mark Twain"—au point Papa, and so noted. Beside the works of Sam Clements, I feather in your "Big Two-Hearted River," a 1930s era short story from the Nick Adams chronicles.

The scent of pine permeates its pages.

This essay is no coming of age account, nor a Zen-like treatise, nor a how-to manual. Simply put, it's simple prose, and simply elegant. No more, no less.

A lone angler begins a reminiscent train ride to a slow cedar-lined Michigan trout stream, disembarks on hard luck terrain, and begins his pilgrimage to the river. Billeted streamside, our angler slips into contemplative currents. A cane rod, a ratchety old reel, tobacco tinned worms, squelchy shoes and a gunny sack as creel meld meditatively, like a Chatham landscape.

Campside, an unadorned flow continues. Tin-cupped coffee, white bread, canned beans and spaghetti stew constitute the principal affairs d' cuisine. Occasionally a brook trout is skilleted.

Lastly, and as always very Hemmingway, light dollops of weather commentary are paged throughout the story.

For reasons never quite clear to me (The tilt of the planet? The pull of the moon?), I'm drawn back to this short sketch. It's the biggest small stream story I've ever known.

This I can say clearly—"Big Two-Hearted" has my heart, and each page runs through it.

# A Frond from Kauai

Poipu Beach. Last midwinter I was lying on a couch, repairing from the dilapidations of life in California. I was reading the Lihue Sports Section. A 3 lb rainbow trout had been caught in a pond at Kokee State Park. It was a new state record.

Bad luck has been synonymous with my Kauai angling exploits. The big game fish I'd hooked in the deep blue off Kauai matched the number I'd caught off the coast of Iowa. None. Yesteryear $500 big game boat rides were reduced to $200 for a "fully guided expedition" for peacock bass in the drinking water reservoir behind Lihue City Hall. Worse, shameless (and illegal I suspect) dusk assaults on the Westin Kauai's Golf Course Ponds for tilapia, the sad looking second cousin of a bluegill, became *de rigueur*. And yet, I could hear Kokee calling me.

With a hopeful heart and a heavy foot I sped up Waimea Canyon towards Kokee that very same morning. Waimea immodestly bills itself as the "Grand Canyon of the Pacific." Precipitation from nearby Mt. Waialeale (550+ inches yearly), said to be "the wettest spot on earth," provides the Kokee Basin streams with their only source of water. All of these streams ultimately flow into the Waimea River.

White hibiscus, banana-like fruit forests and eucalyptus groves border the roadway. And chickens. All the chickens in the known free world. If chickens are your thing, this is your place. Road Island Reds, Speckled Guinea Hens, Bantys, Leghorns—"Crossing the road," flying, roosting, everywhere.

137

Chickens circled my car in the parking lot at Kokee. A large and violent rooster gave me a solid peck. Maybe this rooster was mad because he overslept or thought I was trying to steal a hen. I returned the favor with a rod case to his head. I knocked him into the next week.

The temperature gauge at the park headquarters read 46 degrees. It was chilly (Poipu was about 86 degrees). Grey skies hung over the basin and light raindrops kissed the palm fronds. I was dressed "Full-Luau": aloha shirt, cutoffs, Topsiders, and a straw hat. Flying by the seat of my pants (again) I bought a $7 license, a trail map, and read that the Poomau at Waipoo Falls had the largest concentration of rainbows in the park. I descended into great green trees and purple rocked mountains to the falls, a scant three mile trek downstream.

A mile or so down the trail I met two good natured rifle-toting Hawaiians. The two were pulling a very dead feral pig up the canyon. We exchanged pleasantries and one explained the chicken phenomenon to me. Chicken fights were a gaming sport on the island. Waimea Canyon provided the brood stock.

While departing, the smaller of the two suggested I give up and go back to my car. "Why, the weather?" I asked. He replied, "No Bruddah your reel don't have enough backing."

Waipoo falls is a 6 foot high white throat of water cascading into a pool of undeterminable depth. I opened my fly box, and at first glace it appeared to be inhabited by small tropical birds. By name, these flies are total strangers to me. I tied on a blue and gold Macaw and flicked it out under the falls.

An apple green trout about the size of a cigar hit my fly. I was disappointed in his size and fighting qualities. His cunning however, exceeded his strength and he escaped. The second and last trout I hooked was a solid 12-incher. He headed downstream immediately with me in pursuit. Rocks rounded by time and swift water were my undoing. Fish, rod, reel, and I were headed to the Pacific. Trust in heaven I prayed. I'd like to add that like most folks "my whole life" didn't "flash before me"—just a few highs and a few lows. The pool tailed out and I stood up. I lost (he was probably 18 inches) the trout.

It was nearly 12 noon and I hadn't had a drink yet. The altitude, the inclement weather, and lastly the immersion concluded my trout trip. On the drive down the canyon I began to dream of Hawaiian steel guitars, outriggers, shrouded sacred volcanoes, umbrella drinks, hula girls. I was headed back to paradise!

# Trutta, Trufola & Trebbiano

Long enough ago to be called "once upon a time," Michelangelo Buonarroti, architect, sculptor and painter of the apostolic palace in Rome, ceased his commissioned works. His complaint being that Roman meals were inadequate and indigestible. He demanded sustenance from the Florentine hills: dried trout; truffles (preferably from the base of an oak struck by lightning); and Trebbiano, a white wine. He insisted that procurement of same be placed in the hands of his trusted nephew. Upon receipt and ingestion of same, he deemed the fare "inspirational" and commenced work anew.

Five hundred years later and thirty miles north of Venice I was perched on the high bank side of a Piave River hillock. I was eating a salami sandwich as I watched two paisanos with reel-less telescoping rods fling "mille bugs" (a small white grub) into the soft current. Giovanni, my cousin, once mentioned that riverside risotto farmers augment their incomes (through a generous government subsidy) by raising and releasing rainbow trout for sport fishermen. Shallow stretches of water adjacent to banks and islands are encircled with steel stakes and chicken wire. Trout are released periodically throughout the summer season. The angst of angling for hatchery rainbows left me cold.

Two full turns of the calendar later I'm on the balcony of the Hotel Balestri in Florence overlooking the mellifluous Arno River. Near nightfall, small, apricot-gold lanterned skiffs appear on the waterway. These are eel fishermen. In semi-circle, they worked their nets all night long. A *plenilunio*, the full moon, aided their illumination.

Later that night, in bed, I closed my eyes and got that nice feeling—that just before you fall asleep and know that everything is under control and your body just relaxes feeling. An old latent dream reappeared: a truffled trout with Trebbiano. The morrow's course had been cast.

Enzo, the desk concierge advised me that an afternoon angling opportunity could be easily arranged with his cousin, Luciano, an expert, for a modest amount. The trout could be served that evening in the hotel restaurant.

Luciano, fat, over fifty and nearly finished, was my mirror double. He drove an old grey Fiat sedan. He drove it like it had a Turbo. We drove fifty miles east of Florence to the Alpe di San Benedetto. Here's what I learned about driving in Italy: a red stoplight is not an order—merely a bit of friendly advice; a chrome and metal flying accident is no reason to slow your speed—floor it and drive around; there are no minor injury accidents in Italy, only fatalities; and Italians only pass on curves.

On the Upper Arno, near Bibbiena, we "went local" with the telescoping rods. We baited our hook with a black bug that bit back. No joke. Six eight-inch identically-sized and adipose fin clipped browns were landed. Luciano, an ever artful and expressive Italian would cry—"Naturale!"—"Nativo!"—"Indigeno!"—"Originario!" on each landing. The fix was on and I creeled two hatchery trout for dinner.

Later that evening in the restaurant and well into my second bottle of wine, a white capped chef appeared at my table. With one hand over his heart, he placed a plate of trutta a la trufola before me, and removed his cap with a gracious sweep towards the floor.

I stood up, clicked both heels together sharply, bowed deeply in his direction, swung around towards the plate, genuflected reverently, sat down, and dug in. Another dream down and many more to go.

# For Doug

Riding on the wings of a Horner Deer Hair, size #18, lightly dressed, the aging outdoorsman sped northward on US 101. He would be traveling alone for the first time in nearly twenty-five years. His mentor Doug Merrick, the Maestro, a rod maker Bing Crosby had once called the "Stradivarius of bamboo rodmakers," had succumbed to a respiratory illness that past winter.

Passing the Bay near Candlestick he thought about duck hunting at daybreak and striped bass to a fly at midmorning—a fall ritual for the two. In the city, he reflected on the shop at 475 Third Street where the Maestro conducted business long before the words "fiberglass" and "graphite" entered the angling lexicon.

Doug Merrick was born and raised alongside the Fox River in Wisconsin. Throughout his youth he had a passion for woodworking; fishing rods, golf clubs, pool cue sticks, small animal traps, and snowshoes were his specialties. On graduation day, Doug joined the United States Army Air Corps, a precursor to the Air Force. He was an air crewman in a bomber squadron stationed in England during the Second World War. On a bombing strike over Germany his plane was shot down. He spent two years as a prisoner of war. He was liberated by Russians. Old men, women, and some children with horses pulling cannons attacked the POW camp and the Nazis fled without returning fire. After the war, he returned to Wisconsin and became a game warden. A year later he bought a motorcycle and rode west. He took a job with Standard Oil and worked there until the day he walked into the Winston rod shop on Harrison Street.

At Winston, Doug apprenticed under Winston founder Lou Stoner, an imaginative machinist from Nevada who, at the age of 12, fashioned his first rod from a willow, using spent .22 cartridges as a rod ferrule. A decade earlier Stoner apprenticed Milton "Jimmy" Green on cane rods. Green moved on to develop fiberglass, graphite, boron, and boron/graphite (IM6) rods for the masses. At the time of Lou Stoner's death in 1957, Doug was widely considered to be his equal. Doug later hired and tutored Gary Howells, Jon Tarantino, and on occasion, a very young Steve Rajeff—all GGACC members—to assist in rod production. Jon later went on to design rods at Fisher and then Hardy; Steve went on to design fly rods for Sage and then G. Loomis. They all got their start under Doug Merrick at the Winston rod shop, which by then had moved to its Third Street location.

The shop was perfumed by mothballs and casein glue. The mothballs sat beneath the glass-enclosed fly cases with a hand-lettered sign that read "flies tied by Polly Rosborough, Cal Bird, and Andy Puyans." The Maestro and his Ed McMahon type sidekick, Gary Howells, knocked out about one hundred twenty-five rods per year.

The backroom workshop was a parade, a picnic, really, of colorful characters that dropped by to buy and make rods. Charlie Ritz, the Paris hotelier, came nearly every other year and built a rod or two. Bing Crosby would select a rod before each distant trip to Iceland or Scotland. Crown Prince Axel of Denmark came twice to select salmon rods. The actor Robert "Cannon" Conrad was a regular, along with the highbrow set of San Francisco.

There was the story involving the angling author, Zane Gray, who had received a rod and somehow "forgot" to pay Winston's owner, Lew Stoner, for a rod the Maestro crafted. It was learned that the author was giving a party for his daughter at the Palace Hotel and Stoner put in an appearance and collected, in cash, his stipend. After that, there was a policy change: fifty per cent down and fifty per cent upon receipt. An order for a 7 foot, 3-weight was received in 1955 from 1600 Pennsylvania Avenue, Washington, D.C. The resident, President Eisenhower, was informed that a fifty per cent deposit was required, and, once received, the order would be placed on the waiting list.

Continuing northbound on I-80 and heading for the I-5 turnoff, the driver thought of September dove shoots in Capay Valley, followed up with a smallmouth bass adventure near Guinda in Yolo County. As the great Sacramento Valley and the Sutter Buttes loomed near, the driver reflected on the Maestro in his duck blind, dogless, at eighty plus years of age calling and fetching his own birds. On their last pheasant hunt, the Maestro deadeyed a twenty-seven and three-quarters inch tailed ringneck. Their afternoons were devoted to the small chain of ponds near Elk Creek for Florida largemouths.

The part most remembered? Easy. The soft, slow, sweet golden mornings on Stony Creek, spring and autumn, when the Maestro grace-noted each riffle and glide in the key of B, for bamboo.

# Where Trout Sing

The overture of any angling exercise begins with place. The place in this experience is the Snow Mountain Wilderness, 37,000 acres tucked inside the Mendocino National Forest, 148 miles northeast of the Bay Bridge toll plaza.

Stony Creek is a deep crease between two 7,000-foot mountains: Snow Mountain, and Saint John Mountain. For 14 miles the main fork cataracts downward to its confluence with the south fork at Red Bridge and ultimately to the Sacramento River via a series of pollywog water impoundments.

The creek supports a native population of rainbow trout, a remnant of earlier times when the creek flowed freely to the Sacramento, and these trout returned anadromously as steelhead.

The upper portion of Stony Creek, above Red Bridge, is reserved for catch and release only. Below the bridge five fish can be taken, in season, with a catch and release philosophy adopted for the wintertime.

The upper portion includes all three forks and serves as an incubator for miniature troutlings, who, when sizable, meander downstream to the valley floor below and into a shaded canyon filled with automobile-sized boulders.

In this canyon, the real music begins.

Aside from the north fork campground at Red Bridge, and an old mine road four miles downstream, the creek is inaccessible. The road that parallels the creek quickly elevates to 1,100 feet above the streambed. A yak, and a small Sherpa guide, would be required to navigate these impenetrable canyon sidewalls, along with luck—lots of it.

In early spring intrepid anglers attempt assaults up the creek and are usually beaten back by the runoff, 275 square miles of it, racing swiftly through this narrow chasm. When the water recedes there is no identifiable path, and the inbound angler faces innumerable opportunities to ford. Some swimming and mountainside rappelling are also necessary to complete the trek.

The canyon's floor is carpeted in watercolors, deep green Douglas fir, sky blue lupine, and pasteled mint. Brown bear scat seems to be in evidence nearly everywhere. Yet to actually observe one would require watching them cavort in the Davis Flat campground dumpsters.

They're epicureans.

Rattlesnakes are another matter. Every now and then one will cross your path. They are cordial citizens. They quickly announce their presence when you arrive on a spot, as you even more quickly adios it. Give the reptile his due room, and a fly rod tip prod, and it'll slide away. But cornered—like anything else in nature, it will fight with fury.

There is absolutely no need to embroider any story regarding the size of these fish. A remote, nearly inaccessible location lends itself to all things large. They're happy too, and will gladly welcome you with a wrist wrenching strike.

Maybe, they are so happy—being in that fortified canyon—they sing, and when they do, they sound just like the Mormon Tabernacle Choir.

Back in 1960 Wallace Stegner composed a heartbreakingly beautiful composition to the Outdoor Recreation Resources Committee. Over time, it would come to be called The Wilderness Letter. He eloquently, and descriptively, maintains the essential need of man's heart and soul for wilderness. He concludes his treatise with this phrase: that we are or should all be a part of the "geography of hope" to maintain and extend wilderness.

I have a hope too—that the folks at Fish and Game and CalTrout include this watershed in their wild trout waters, because it is—and I hope it always will be.

# On a Golden Pond

Last mid-century Charlie McDermand penned a novella entitled *Waters of the Golden Trout Country*. This was a "how-to" book, encapsulating all the Eastern Sierra routes to the 24-karat trout.

In that place and during that time our backpack equipment consisted of surplus WWII knapsacks and mummy bags. A genuine Trapper Nelson hickory wood frame appeared in the early '50s and was *de rigueur* for the Sierra Club set.

This time I speak of entered my consciousness long before the word "ecology" and the phrases "catch & release" and "environmental impact" appeared. The closest a human being could get to a lunar-like landscape were these barren ridges and cirques. Man had not yet been to the moon.

McDermand's notes were our Bible. This religion was my religion, and our gang attended services for thirty or more summers.

Sonora pass north of Yosemite usually opens in May. My tribe would usually cross over same in May and hustle down #395 to Bishop and acclimatize ourselves to the high mountain altitude for a day. This training usually consisted of free-weight curls at the Antler Tavern on Main and an early a.m. rising to put the empty pizza boxes in the motel dumpster. Watching the joggers run by was our cardio workout.

Fortified, we tackled Whitney Portal, Pine Creek, Kearsarge and my beloved Piute Pass, gateway to the Ansel Adams Wilderness area.

The two hundred acre Desolation Lake rests at an altitude of 11,381 feet in the northeast corner of Fresno County. It is accessed by Piute Pass west of Bishop at North Lake and is a fourteen mile loop in and out. USGS Mt. Goddard and Mt. Tom will get you in and out with ease. McDermand said it has the largest Goldens in the Sierras. It did and does. I was an early sucker for this lake and a repeater. To the best of my recollection, which should never be taken for gospel, there are no sardine class trout in this lake. The meadow areas adjacent to the inlet and outlets have big-uns that could go 2½ to 3 inches between the eyes. I hooked but never landed these brutes. McDermand claims these submarines are in the 4 to 8 pound range. I've landed legitimate 18-inchers with a solid 15-inch average.

Should you go, you'll be alone, except for the marmots, badger-like thieves who invade camp as quickly as Sitting Bull did Custer. Lock up the goods. I have a hard time saying this, and weigh my words lightly, my flask disappeared on one such occasion.

Coming down off the mountains you'll probably want to take a good soak in Hot Creek State Park. It's free. This watercress creek is a constant 90 degrees. The thermals and sand spouts will suspend you in mid water much like a piece of fruit in Jell-O.

Lastly, most folks would wonder why an angler, any angler, would provide honest information on a sweet spot. Simple. I won't be going back; I won't be going back. Our state motto, "Men to match my mountains" no longer applies to me. In youth, we think all things are possible. But at an older age, we are unable or unsure of ourselves.

So this chapter of my life stream concludes and I offer it to you, my brothers and sisters of this great angling fraternity. This is the only good golden trout story I know and what a good story it is.

# Fading Light

The family had dwindled down to two, herself and her son. Her fading life was being written by her bedroom window, the one she watched the world through. The good earth from afar, a star, a summer sunset or a white winter moon rise were blossoms of good conversation between the two. That, and the notion of her on an ocean voyage somewhere, anywhere, sometime soon.

Her son watched her read travel books, study maps, and chart a course that only her heart would ever steer. Oftentimes she peppered her conversation with a nauticalness that puzzled him. Perhaps in another place and time she had been a seaman. In this one, she had never seen an ocean or had the olfactory scent of salt sea air. Maybe his blessed mother had met Melville in another life. Lord knows she never objected to swigs of the strong stuff or glittering streaks of profanity. She had come to be an able-bodied sailor, so to speak, who had never seen the sea.

His mother had an optimistic attitude towards everything on earth, and as spring sprang, she suggested he go out fishing and let spring surprise him again. He didn't. His logic was simple, his mother had become his child, with all responsibilities for her welfare resting on his shoulders.

There are those, she once said, who live a life of self pity and regret over an unlived life; she was not one of them. She had lived a good life, and on her road to eternity she would welcome seeing family, old friends, and to a lesser extent, a favorite pet or two.

Parents become our anchors here on earth, and when one leaves, an unmooring occurs. The "theys" say that if you leave in your sleep you've lived a good life, and so it happened that way. In late spring she disembarked.

"All living things must leave" she once said, "It's the natural order of things to move over and make room for the new crew coming in." It left him rudderless.

Time and distance are always absolute antidotes. Summer slipped by, and each day he seemed stronger. He no longer needed a nightly blast of bourbon to run through his veins like the immediate blast of stun gun to numb himself to sleep. And more importantly, he got back in touch with an old friend. Himself.

Towards twilight one fall evening he drove his car on an old dirt road to a bend in the river, his place, where trout jumped as though they were on trampolines. He reached for his fly rod and walked through a red and gold apple orchard. Windfall apples were all about, and a light breeze whispered through the trees. When he reached the streamside he sat down and went inside himself, again. He thought about the odds and ends, the bits and pieces of their lives that added up through the years, their souvenirs.

On the opposite side of the river a small rivulet entered. When spring runoff came late, and later receded, small blue and white wild flowers dotted the floodplain. *Myosotis* flowers, commonly called forget-me-nots.

There was melancholy in his mood and a tear appeared. He imagined his mother at the helm of a ship, with a new set of sails on a following sea. "Shiver me timbers" he thought, "She's sailing somewhere." And in the fading light, the twilight, he closed his eyes and he never stopped smiling.

# Fifty Fish

The big river valley was white. He was sitting, watching a light skein of snow fall outside his kitchen window. He liked looking out over this landscape, much like someone staring at a fire afterglow going out of control. While he watched, he wondered.

He felt that if it were possible to see deep inside his heart, there was truly no sad part.

At one time he thought, as some folks sometimes do, that there may be a book in him. That thought passed quickly though. It would be impossible for him to write a forlorn ode to an unlived life, a sad love song, or despair over aging. He was here at a good time, and having a good time while he was here. And with any luck at all, a few more fish would follow. It would be a while though, the blacks, browns and greys of winter would need to chameleon green.

In his mind, all the great mental souvenirs of his life and times were about the Bay, San Francisco Bay. This is how it had always been.

His earliest remembrances were watching others fish. He watched his father fish, an uncle fish, family friends fish. There was no toy tackle back then. The child-sized Snoopy rod and reel deal of today had not yet come into being, and for that matter, neither had Snoopy.

And so it was that he watched, and watched others until he could muster up enough muscle to cast a line into great depths of San Francisco Bay, approximately seven feet from the shoreline.

His first angling accouterments were acquired at low water, picking snagged sinkers and hooks off pier pilings, clumps of kelp, or from between rocks. He would present his cache to his father who nodded an affectionate approval at his worthless "gear."

His first tackle box was a cigar box. Cigar boxes were all over in those days. The preferred model was the "Cubano Long." Its contents would rise like a river and recede like an outgoing tide.

He loved to bait fish back then. Bits of bait fish like smelt, shiners, and pile worms cast across small shoals, an inlet, an effluent discharge, or tidal confluences rewarded him with redtail perch, sharks, stingrays, but never, ever, the elusive (to him) striped bass. "That fish will come to you later on in life" his father would add. And just as his father said, they did.

There was no easy explanation for what happened next. He placed a pen in hand, and the pad that was used for groceries before him, and he began to write to no one in particular:

"I wish to place on record that a day filled with a fifty fish catch is of no concern to me, a mere matter. Allow me to angle for one large one, anywhere. The hook set, the struggle, or its landing would be of little consequence. The worth, and the weight of that fish would be measured in the warmth of my winter dreams."

When he finished he looked up and out the window. The snowfall had swerved to falling water-rain. He, of course, was safe and warm inside, and feeling like Faulkner.

# December 21st

Silver Sirius, the brightest star illuminating the California night was extinguishing itself like a Roman Candle that had burned bright and fast. Darkness was giving way to lightness, a new dawn, on a new day.

Up in the north state, mandarin orange rays were advancing up the Cascade range. Yellow, red and brown leaves speckled the pools and riffles of the Warner Range. Redside rainbows finned, trance-like in the Pit River headwaters and its East Creek Branch. It was blue cold. Further down the Cascades, Lake Almanor lay motionless. Its non-native brown trout launching themselves into cursory spawning forays up the Hamilton Branch and the North Fork of the Feather River.

Down Tahoe way the Kokanee salmon were huddling up at the mouth of Taylor Creek, awaiting what comes naturally. Further down the Truckee River Basin, Paiute and Lahonton cutthrout trout were making plans for the same assault up river. South of Tahoe, the high Sierra mountains had been brushed with a light skein of snow, and its over-fished and under-nourished golden trout were looking for what was left over from the ever encroaching, ever colorful eastern brook trout.

The sun's ray's peeked up and over the mountains in the great valleys and warmed away curdled grey clouds. The valley's reservoir and river residents appreciated it. The smallmouth and largemouth bass of Lake Shasta began gorging on threadfin shad, while the two major river veins in the valley received a precocious run of undersized and over-sexed stripers. Down around the Delta, green and white sturgeon waited patiently for the winter herring to come in and drop their eggs, time for one last feast before they galloped upstream to spawn.

It was late afternoon as an ebbing sun still shined over the Northern California coastline at Eureka. Dungeness crabs were hurdling themselves into crab traps for want of a sardine head. The Klamath and Trinity Rivers had already received the greatest bulk of their runs; what remained was for the smaller North Coast streams to swell, recede to grey-green, and then, and only then, would the native steelhead and salmon return home.

On San Francisco Bay a changing of the guard was taking place. On piers, peninsulas and promontories, fisherman who held true to the incoming tide as best were being replaced by those who subscribed to the theory that the outgoing tide was better.

Out near the Golden Gate, on the Pacific escarpment, the sun slipped down below the horizon. The solstice, the day, and another story had completed.

# *Naturalness*

Back in the '40s when we were young, when our worlds were young, our lives seemed simple and uncomplicated. It seemed as though all things were possible and within easy reach.

Everything, and every item we used seemed free of pretension and artificiality.

Like the sporting life, and sporting goods for instance.

You could count on those venerable American companies like Wilson, or Spaulding, to produce a product that once placed in your hands was readily identifiable as baseball bat of Tennessee ash, or a baseball mitt—hand-sewn and strung together with Texas leather—ready to receive a genuine horsehide baseball. Gridiron accoutrements like footballs were made from pigskins, and helmets from roughout leather. Athletic shoes were created from one hide or another. The blue flowered flax plant rendered to liquid was reincarnated as linseed oil that softened and prolonged the life of these leather goods. Byproducts all, compliments of Mother Nature, naturally.

Boats, mostly bay boats were hand crafted by Anderson and Cristofani of San Francisco. You could buy a small skiff, a sailboat, or a Monterrey trawler. Despite their size differences, these watercraft were all pedigreed in the same fashion. Oregon Port Orford cedar for side planking, anchored to ribbing and decking of California oak. This was the accepted coastal standard, unless your vessel was ocean rated.

If you wanted to fish the big blue out at Ocean Beach you bought a length of imported Calcutta cane from a bait shop for a buck. Line guides, one of red agate if you had the dough, were secured to the cane with a Philippine hemp fiber. The cane was then "shellacked" with an alcohol-based varnish for waterproofing. An aluminum "c" clamp secured your reel to the rod with two wing nuts, and you were in business.

A Tonkin cane fly rod with a Portuguese cork grip, or a split bamboo bait casting rod was usually purchased at a sporting goods store, or more commonly at a hardware store. The rod racks back then served double duty; cane rods were interspersed with repeating rifles and shotguns with fine-grain American walnut stocks. Wicker creels made of willow with embossed leather trim and straps were displayed beside smooth silk fly lines and catgut leaders. Furs for fly tying were common deer, elk, seal, muskrat, rabbit, and polar bear. Feathers from free-flying fowl and ducks completed the assortment.

The Bean and Bauer catalogs of then and now are separate species. No pictures of smiling backpackers prancing over sunlit mountaintops were in evidence. Nope, not at all. You could find expedition grade gear; eider down jackets, a south pole rated sleeping bag, or a sherpa tested backpack. You had your choice of colors also; cotton fatigue green, and cotton fatigue green. Or, you could go to the local Army-Navy Surplus stores that dotted San Francisco and buy a near-new canvas duck tent, a wool jacket, or a military mess kit like most California outdoorsmen did back then.

Back then, it was safe to conclude that nearly all of our sporting good paraphernalia was obtained from an innate living thing or natural object.

Around 1950 our worlds were rocked with the synthetic age. An age of wonder so to speak as we were introduced to Wonder Bread, Wondra Flour, and the fiberglass Wonderod by Shakespeare—all wonderful new products and materials for making the sporting life and sporting goods carefree. Wooden boats became aluminum. Gunstocks, plastic; baseball bats, aluminum; gloves, plastic and nylon; shoes, ungenuine unborn naugahyde; clothing, nylon and rayon. Synthetics all, with no soul. Not James Brown soul, or fillet of sole, or shoe sole, but the intrinsic soul and essence of a god given organic creation that evolved through nature, not from some chemist's test tube. "Better living through chemistry" was a nationally televised slogan, and we took the bait.

To an old timer, a weathered creel with fern remnants inside imparts a more acceptable fragrance than "Evening in Paris" perfume, a pleasant reminiscence of far flung fields and free flowing streams. The ratchety old single action fly reel, the one where the drag never worked well, has been replaced by today's titanium "atom splitting option" fly reel. To remove a tattered cane rod from its venerable old canvas sack recollects the time you brought that varnished beauty home and uncased it at every convenience, for no reason at all. Your fly rod's caked cork grip, with a silver scaled speck or two recalls the one, perhaps two, significant fish you caught in your life. Those sporting items were natural extensions of ourselves, and our lives. All regrettably reduced to garage relics and storeroom fossils.

Those old sporting goods that we held in our hands, cradled in our arms and carried on our backs over far flung fields, through deep forests, and over wide open waters served us so well, so long ago. To an old sportsman, our old gear meant as much to us as the Queen does to England.

Often times, it seems as though we cannot go back to those places, those times, and those things that meant so much to us way back when, unless, unless we close our eyes and dream. Naturally.

www.ingramcontent.com/pod-product-compliance
Lightning Source LLC
Chambersburg PA
CBHW030417100426
42812CB00028B/2996/J